LONG VOYAGE OUT OF WAR

CH00694881

This trilogy of plays about the effect[s] protagonist at different times and dif[...] commissioned by BBC Television, is [...] It succeeds in illuminating the moder[...] of war through the skilful delineation [...] relationships. It has been described a[...] [...] this scale and magnitude of subject has been attempted on television" in the field of original TV drama and "a hope for the new kind of civilisation into which we are moving". Its awareness of man's elemental relationship to land, time and sea give it a Shakespearean scope.

The first play in the volume, The Gentle Invasion, subtly evokes the atmosphere and spirit of a rural Kentish community at the outbreak of World War II. The people, by a false alarm, think the expected German invasion of 1940 is actually commencing. It shows the fabric of that centuries-old civilisation starting to change and then disintegrate under the stresses and exigencies of an invasion that finally comes from within.

Battle at Tematangi is set in the Philippines in 1954, and finds Turk, the protagonist of the first play, caught up in a Spanish Civil War type of revolution, to determine what new form society should take. It shows the same skill in recapturing a particular society at a particular time, through detailed psychological characterisation and by a profound richness of humour that is always precisely to the point. Ironically, it is through straying into the fallout of the first Bikini H-bomb test that the group of mercenaries of which Turk is one discovers how to live together on a new basis.

The Last Enemy, which completes the trilogy, is set in 1976. Turk is now in late-middle age, and the play centres on his conflict as an idealist between trying to help society as a whole, now launching forward on its new basis, and trying to help a sick individual within it. Its picture of the gradual curing of an autistic child, and the trilogy's calm resolution of hope and a guarded optimism for mankind, are profoundly moving.

PLAYSCRIPT 54

'long voyage out of war'

A TRILOGY OF TELEVISION PLAYS:
THE GENTLE INVASION
BATTLE AT TEMATANGI
THE LAST ENEMY

ian curteis

CALDER AND BOYARS · LONDON

First published in Great Britain 1971 by
Calder and Boyars Limited
18 Brewer Street, London W1R 4AS

All performing rights in these plays are strictly reserved and
applications for performances should be made to:
Richard Hatton Limited
17a Curzon Street   London W 1

No performance of these plays may be given unless a licence has
been obtained prior to rehearsal.

ISBN 0 7145 0783 0 Cloth Edition
ISBN 0 7145 0784 9 Paper Edition

Printed by photo-lithography
and made in Great Britain at
The Pitman Press, Bath

For Joan

I owe most particular thanks to James Brabazon who, as script editor of the old Theatre 625 programme on BBC-2, commissioned this trilogy and was a tower of wisdom, guidance, understanding and practical help during the two years of its writing;

to Barbara Furneaux, Principal of The Lindens, a Surrey County Council unit for severely disturbed, psychotic and autistic children, and a leading authority in this country for their treatment; to her staff and the children under her care, for their very great help and understanding during the writing of the autistic child in the third play;

to Mark Shivas, Shaun MacLoughlin and Rob Knights, the producer, editor and director of the programme; to the leading actors, cameramen, designers, technicians and many others, for their infinite patience and dedication during the six months of the production and recording.

The trilogy was written 1966-8, recorded in 1970 and transmitted in 1971.

The texts that follow are the full and proper versions, which had to be cut for production to fit their transmission slots on BBC-2.

Ian Curteis

LONG VOYAGE OUT OF WAR

EDITOR'S NOTE

As these are television plays, dependent for their effect on the flow from one image to another and from one scene to the next, the system of marking directions and the divisions between scenes and acts differs from other Playscripts.

The key is as follows:

(1) Dashes placed between sentences in the directions indicate changes of image.

(2) An asterisk placed at the beginning of a line denotes a change of scene.

(3) A horizontal line printed across the page denotes the end of one act and the beginning of the next.

(4) Occasionally, brackets are placed round clusters of dialogue with the words 'simultaneously' (or 'sim.') or 'overlapping' outside them. For those readers unfamiliar with television terminology, 'simultaneously' in this context means all the characters speaking at once, 'overlapping' means one character cutting into the other's speech, thus giving a montage effect to an extended section of dialogue.

This sytem, which dispenses with titles like ACT ONE or Scene One, will help the reader to imagine the trilogy in televisual terms as he reads it, rather than as something adapted from the theatre.

Jonathan Hammond

CONTENTS

THE GENTLE INVASION

THE GENTLE INVASION was first presented on BBC-2
Television, January 27th, 1971, with the following cast:

TURK GODFRAY	Mike Pratt
DOD IPPS	Dan Meaden
ANDY IPPS	Ken Jones
OLD'UN WILLIAMS	Godfrey Quigley
MRS. PRIDDY	Susan Richards
BOY GODFRAY	Rufus Frampton
ESSIE GODFRAY	Gabrielle Hamilton
FRANK GODFRAY	John Barrett
PETER PRICE	Leon Vitali
CHRISTINE PRICE	Susan Williamson
SAMBO HARTHOG	Bloke Modisane
MRS. TRAFFORD	Florence Allsworth
MR. TRAFFORD	Bart Allison

The play was produced by Mark Shivas.
The play was directed by Robert Knights.

(Romney Marsh, Kent. September 1940. 3.30 a.m.

Darkness. Closeup a rusty coastguard klaxon, pulsing out
shrill alarm blasts: tilt up to low night cloud, heavy with
rain. The deep throb of thousands of aircraft is heard,
crossing steadily over into England. (Sound continues under:)
/ An upstairs window bursts open: FRANK GODFRAY throws
out armfuls of soft possessions onto the dirt track outside. /
A teenage couple, the girl seven months pregnant, loading
essential possessions onto a small handcart - PETER and
CHRISTINE PRICE. They work silently, very frightened,
coats over their nightclothes. / ANDY IPPS pounds heavily
down the stairs of his cottage, pulling on his clothes, and
running outside. / A whitehaired woman, holding up a lamp,
peers through a steamy pane in her kitchen window. Her
name is MRS. PRIDDY. / Darkness. / OLD'UN WILLIAMS,
an immense man in his late sixties, standing quite still in
the fields, listening. Zoom in on his face. / Cattle restless
in the grey gloom, thudding their hooves. Flocks of sheep
running and veering round in huge sweeps of movement
through the wet grass. / A tractor roars into life in a
corrugated iron tractor-shelter. FRANK GODFRAY strikes
a match inside, and runs across, shielding the flame. /
Three big church bells in a tiny mediaeval belfry, swinging
and clashing erratically. (Sound continues under:) / A
family of three, MOTHER 50, sons of 25 and 13 - TURK and
THE BOY - hastily loading essentials onto a rough dogcart.
TURK is in crumpled khaki uniform. They shout at each
other. THE BOY is excited and laughs. / DOD IPPS sits
beside his bed, listening, very frightened. His room is cold
and bare. / Closeup the bells, erratic, urgent. The klaxon
continues in the distance.

This is Old Romney, a hamlet in the centre of Romney Marsh,
Kent: once a village, it now has only six inhabited houses and
an immensely-thick-walled, tiny, clumsy, Saxon church.
Other houses stand in ruins. The hamlet is an island in the
thousands of acres of flat, bleak, but rich, old pasture: and,
bounding three sides of that, the sea.

A plane drops into view out of the cloud and

13

appears to hover for a moment, silent: then it dips and
moves slowly towards us, swooping and diving, its noise
growing to a scream./ People pause and look up.

*An elderly couple in bed together: brown photos, faded table
covers: silence in the room./ Outside, the plane approaches./
They lie awake, their eyes wide open.

OLD WOMAN. (whispering) Listen!

*(DOD IPPS throws open his window and looks./ People stare
transfixed at the approaching plane./ ANDY IPPS runs across
the single street)

ANDY. Well then?

FATHER. (at tractor) Inside!

TURK. (to MRS. PRIDDY) Light!

MOTHER. What?

FATHER. Go on!

(He runs for them)

MRS. PRIDDY. (at her door) Hey!

TURK. (shout) Light, put out your light!

FATHER. Get in quick, get inside!

BOY. Look at it!

MOTHER. I told you so, didn't I? (THE FATHER bundles them
in) Didn't I tell you so?

TURK. Your light, you stupid old bag!

MRS. PRIDDY. (taking a step out, and leaving her door open)
Hey!

(TURK runs across and shoves her into the house, turning
out the light, and bustling her under the sink. She squawks
protestingly./ DOD IPPS runs downstairs two at a time,
jumping the last flight at a bound./ The young husband pushes
his wife uncertainly into the house, his eyes on the plane./
DOD and ANDY IPPS run across the yard and jump into a

14

ditch, flattening themselves against its banks)

*(The Beale living room. The family enter in a panic)

(FATHER. Sofa, behind the sofa, get down. Arms over your) simultaneously
(head.   )
(   )
(MOTHER. We should have gone last week when I said, they)
(warned us.   )

BOY. Where's Turk?

FATHER. Down, get down boy -

MOTHER. - I said so, didn't I?

FATHER. - against the wall, the wall, that's what they said.
    Grip with your feet -

(MOTHER. Didn't I say so?   )
(   ) simultaneously
(FATHER. - arms over your head!   )

BOY. (doing so) Turk?

    (They tense themselves, screwing up their faces)

*(PETER and CHRISTINE stand halfway up the stairs of their
    house. The scream of the plane is deafening)

CHRISTINE. (shouting) Well?

    (PETER shivers)

    Well?

    *(The fields outside the hamlet: OLD'UN walking and stumbling
    through the grass, looking up at the plane, walking towards
    it, as if hypnotised by it)

    *(The elderly couple in bed. The plane's yell cuts the ears./
    The old man is terrified, brittle stick-arms rigidly holding
    him up from the bed in anticipation./The old woman lies
    back, relaxed, almost smiling)

    *(The bomb falls, a shrill crack followed by a grating boom.
    Windows are blown in, outbuildings and ceilings collapse.
    The terrible sound of solid brick walls shuddering and ripping

15

like thick calico. /Closeup shots of great cracks and
rifts in brickwork, stone wall, trees, the earth: rapidly
panning up and along these rifts and splittings, some of them
still opening as we see them, mixing between them. / The
reflection of flames and smoke: the sounds of shouting and
running, a horse screaming in pain and cattle heavily pounding
past./ People run, clamber and stumble from shelter: rapid
jerky shots: some stand dazed and indecisive, others panic
and run. / A second plane is heard approaching. The women
scream, and run towards the thickwalled church)

(They enter the church, which is dark and tiny. A votive
light is just seen, and in the dimness the vast rough
buttresses and huge piles of timber which have accumulated
over the years to prop the place up and hold it together./ They
brace themselves against the walls. The scream of the second
plane is making the whole place vibrate./ The bomb falls,
just outside: a heavy crack quickly followed by the cataclysmic,
headfilling shout of the explosion, stabbing like sudden
violent earache: the four-foot-thick walls they brace on for
support give a sickening lift, lurch and shudder: the whole
mass of the building groans and moves appallingly on its
foundations, as if the entire world around them was
agonisingly changing its shape./ Instant darkness: shouting
and screaming)

(There is a tremendous hail of stonework, rubble, brickwork
and heavy masonry from the roof. The air fills with thick
lungclogging filth and stonedust./ A torch fallen on the floor
gives glimpses of swirling dust, filth, people running about
or lying injured and in pain, and further falls of masonry
from the roof. The torch is kicked and knocked and we see
in rapid turns, panic, shouting, fear, pain, violence and
struggle)

(FATHER. Light! Let's have your light! (to DOD IPPS) Get)
(out of the road, man, get out... dust!...   )
(   )
(TURK. Hold it, hold it! Let's have that light then, for Christs)
(sake... (fit of coughing)...   )
(   )
(OLD'UN. Back then! (tremendous roar) Keep under this end,)
(get against it, under the edge.   )
(   )
(BOY. Light!...where's the... can't see...   )
(   )
(ANDY IPPS. Back then, towards him, you can hear him, move)
(then! Just feel your way, move, go on, move -   )

simultaneously

16

(THE BOY suddenly screams with pain, topping this:)

BOY. Ah!....Jesus Jesus...

(MOTHER. (screaming on his cry of pain) Something come) simultaneously
(down on him Turk, help him, there's something...)
( )
(TURK. There's someone hurt, there, someone hurt. Get)
(off, get off! - right, have that then! (sound of blow))
(Christ for some light! -)
( )
(FATHER. All right, alright woman, shut up, shut it!)

(The votive lamp swings violently back and forth in a wide
arc in the darkness, striking fallen beams and masonry
and recoiling, still alight)

(OLD'UN. Where - where is he? Where's the boy? (fit of) simultaneously
(coughing) Light! Get hold of yourself, get hold!)
( )
(MOTHER. Help him, help him, where is he? Boy?)
( )
(ANDY IPPS. Feel your way then! Don't move ahead till)
(you feel - don't touch him -)

(DOD IPPS is on his hands and knees, sobbing and rocking
backwards and forwards rapidly)

MRS. PRIDDY. (stands dazed, giving a strange high quiet cry)
Oh...oh...oh...God...God...

(CHRISTINE is sobbing hysterically)

PETER. (ineffectually) Stop it! Up this way here, the far end
- Quiet, can't you, stop that!

(He half carries her to the tower end of the nave)

(The grating roar of the collapse finishes: chunks of masonry
still continue to fall from the roof. TURK and THE OLD'UN
are bawling at each other in near-pitch blackness)

TURK. - he's hurt, the boy's hurt! -

OLD'UN. Don't stir then, you'll knock into him, don't stir till
I say -

ANDY. Get on, lad, do like he says, not -

17

OLD'UN. (stopping TURK with a roar) Don't stir! This is my place chick, I call the tune round here, you're just a bloody joke boy! -

(We see MRS. PRIDDY, calling dazed:)

MRS. PRIDDY. Where are you then, eh? I can hear you but ...what's the matter, eh? Boy?

BOY. (faintly, out of vision) I split... I split my shoulder.

(FATHER. Over there. All right son, we're with you...)
(   )
(TURK. Watch him then, mind him, the kids hurt, he's hurt -) simultaneously
(   )
(OLD'UN. All right lad. (shouts) Hold your noise, shut it!)
(Where is he? Boy? Boy?   )
(   )
(MOTHER. Over here, Frank, look near me, towards me...)

(They are heard stumbling about in the dark. The camera imitates their actions, picking out vague shadows and shapes)

(Tower end of the nave: CHRISTINE sobs noisily)

PETER. Alright, darling, it's alright, alright, there now -

FATHER. Shut her up, can't you, can't you keep her quiet?

PETER. (suddenly yelling) I'm trying to, aren't I?

(CHRISTINE shrieks anew)

TURK. (topping - shout) Hold your noise!

FATHER. (suddenly) Torch, here's a torch!

(TURK. Well, let's be having it then! -)
(   )
(MOTHER. Put it on, put it on!   ) simultaneously
(   )
(ANDY. Come on with it then -   )

(MRS. PRIDDY finds THE BOY huddled in a smashed box pew)

MRS. PRIDDY. Alright, boyey, we're here now, we're here

18

my bird.

OLD'UN. (calling at a distance) Alright, lad, hurt are you? Where is he?

TURK. (at a distance) No - over there, that way.

ANDY. Here mister -

MRS. PRIDDY (close) What is it, what you done to yourself, eh?

TURK. Here, here he is!

OLD'UN. (finding him) Ah!

MOTHER. Is he there? Got him?

OLD'UN. Keep off missis, keep away till we see.

MOTHER. But we've got to -

ANDY. Keep off like he says.

MOTHER. Torch! Frank! - where's that... must see!

FATHER. (wrestling with torch) I can't... I can't...

(DOD IPPS, leaning against the wall, his face in a fever of sweat, moans high -)

DOD. Ah.......

TURK. (with boy) He's on his face. Help him round, help him.

MRS. PRIDDY. Boy?

OLD'UN. Something here, across him -

TURK. Let's come - move -

(Tower end of the nave)

PETER. All right?

CHRISTINE. (nods mutely, white)

PETER. No pains?

CHRISTINE. (shakes her head)

(Nave)

MOTHER. (to FATHER, wrestling for the torch) Give it me.
  Give it!

OLD'UN. ... must have fainted.

TURK. Blood here I think.

MRS. PRIDDY. (sob)

TURK. (suddenly, excitedly) It's a beam, a beam from the
  roof over his chest! Grab hold, grab hold -

OLD'UN. Can't see! - (THE BOY whimpers) Alright lad -

TURK. (to his parents) Move, then, move!

MOTHER. It won't... won't bloody...!

  (In her exasperation she bangs it against the pulpit steps)

OLD'UN. (close to BOY) Hurt your shoulder, have you?
  - let's feel then -

TURK. (to OLD'UN) Come on, get hold -

OLD'UN. Don't stir, there's a torch coming, just hold it a -

TURK. It's across his chest, mate, across his chest! -

  (Dust swirls across)

MRS. PRIDDY. He's not moving!

TURK. (with feverish speed) Dad look, grab hold, we'll shift
  this bastard beam -

OLD'UN. (shout) When we can see we'll raise it, if we try in
  the glim we'll not -

20

TURK. OK Dad? - right...

(OLD'UN. You can't, it weighs a ton boy -   )
(   )
(FATHER. Don't want to do anything that would risk -) sim
(   )
(ANDY. Do what he says lad!   )

MRS. PRIDDY. (shielding THE BOY from them)... mind, mind
...

OLD'UN. Put it down, remember the lad, remember the boy -

TURK. What in hell do you think I'm doing! -

    (TURK's MOTHER, struggling with the torch, raises her
    head and shouts with exasperation)!

FATHER. Quick woman!

TURK. Grab hold then and - hup! -

(OLD'UN. Keep off him, he can't do it by himself -   )
(   ) sim
(ANDY IPPS. (to MRS. PRIDDY) Mind it missis, watch)
(yourself, watch it -   )

    (The torch suddenly comes on, illuminating TURK in a
    superhuman struggle to get the beam off THE BOY by
    himself. He has raised it only about two inches clear of THE
    BOY's chest)

((OLD'UN. Bloody madman, I - here, over here -   ))
((   ))
((ANDY. What'y're doing, you -   ))
((   ))
((PETER. (jumps up and runs in)   )) simultaneously
((   ))
((CHRISTINE. Peter!   ))
((   ))
((MRS. PRIDDY. (seeing THE BOY's chest) Oh - oh where))
((it is, where... I think he's... (goes to touch him)))
((   ))
((MOTHER. Don't touch him, don't touch him!   ))

OLD'UN. Down, boy, put it down, lay it down!

MRS. PRIDDY. Please, please -

FATHER. Give me hold -

(He and ANDY IPPS move to take it)

OLD'UN. This end!

TURK. (kicking at them with one foot) Get off; take your
bleeding hands off -

MOTHER. (shout) Watch him! -

OLD'UN. Mind it woman - (pulls MRS. PRIDDY clear) -

ANDY. Torch steady!

TURK. MIND!.... (preparing to swing it) Mind!...

PETER. (meekly) Can I help?

(A sudden movement in the wall above and behind them)

DOD. Mind the wall, the wall - (he points)

```
(TURK. Move him then, move him, quick - )
(                                       )
(OLD'UN. Hold it there, keep it there - )
(                                       ) sim.
(ANDY. Can't see - move yourself -      )
(                                       )
(MOTHER. (screams)                      )
```

(A noise of splitting and grating: a huge beam swings
free from the roof and hangs suspended. A further fall of
stone and dust)

```
(TURK. The roof! Watch out, I'm going to swing it over )
(    and - hu! -                                        )
(                                                       )
(OLD'UN. Lay it down, lay the thing down - (fit of coughing) )
(                                                       )
(MOTHER. Pull him back, pull the boy clear, forget the )
(    beam -                                             )
(MRS. PRIDDY. Don't, don't move him! -                 )
(                                                       )
(ANDY. Put it down then, down lad -                    )
```
simultaneously

(TURK swings and throws the beam to one side, clear of THE
BOY)

OLD'UN. (gives a cry that cuts through the end of this fall)
Ah!...

(Pause. Silence)

(They are all coughing and choking heavily. The filth and
dust are starting to settle: the collapse is over./ There is a
sudden fizz and flare of light: they all look up blinking./
DOD is lighting a thick altar candle in the wrecked chancel)

ANDY IPPS. Thank the Lord for that.

FATHER. (croaking) Over here - let's have it - here -

TURK. (spluttering and coughing) Right old peasouper, innit?
(sings) "Smoke gets in your eyes"...

OLD'UN. Shut up.

TURK. Only having a bit of a singsong, that's all, cheer us all
up a bit -

OLD'UN. (coughing) Shut up.

TURK. You're not musical, that's your trouble. You'll never
be Forces Sweetheart.

(DOD, in the chancel, is peering about with the candle)

DOD. No-one here, nothing...

FATHER. (to him) Hey!

ANDY. (looking up) Let's have it!

(PETER and CHRISTINE: tower end of the nave)

CHRISTINE. How many...where are those old people?

PETER. What?

CHRISTINE. You know - next door to us; where are they?

(Nave)

DOD. (pulling a jacket from the rubble) It's a coat, someone's coat. (holds it up) John's, this is.

TURK. Dod!

FATHER. Blust man!

BOY. (whimpers)

(OLD'UN. Bring it!)
( ) sim.
(ANDY. Light, Doddy!)

(Tower end of the nave)

CHRISTINE. Ten of us.

PETER. Yea?

(Nave)

FATHER. Sick

MOTHER. (out of vision) Dod!

TURK. Yea.

DOD. (very dazed) And where are the others?

(OLD'UN. Light, bring it, the boy's hurt!)
( ) sim.
(ANDY. (crossing to him) For God's sake, you great)
(stupid -)

DOD. (note of hysteria) Where's Mr. Trafford? - eh? - and George Stanley, where's John?

TURK. Move!

OLD'UN. Get it.

ANDY. (snatching it) Give it here.

DOD. But where -

OLD'UN. Shut it!

DOD. What -

OLD'UN. SHUT it!

DOD. (launching forward) I don't -

   (ANDY IPPS slaps him across the face.)

   (Tower area)

CHRISTINE. They couldn't have... they couldn't have...?

   (She looks at PETER, fright dawning)

   (Nave area. Silence. Close-up in turn, ANDY IPPS, MRS.
   PRIDDY, TURK, THE MOTHER and THE FATHER, looking
   down at OLD'UN's examination of THE BOY, their faces lit
   by the candle)

FATHER. He alright, mister?

OLD'UN. Don't know. He's breathing, any rate. No blood,
   but you can't tell, could be something internal.

   (THE MOTHER rises, barely holding back her repulsion and
   crosses away from THE BOY to by CHRISTINE and PETER)

CHRISTINE. (to her - frightened) Where are the others?

BOY. (whimpers with pain)

FATHER. Alright son -

BOY. Ah -

FATHER. Alright son, its alright, you had a bit of an accident,
   that's all -

BOY. Oh, it's you, Dad. I was ... I was dreaming about this
   woman.

TURK. Don't waste time, do he? -

FATHER. Hurt, does it?

TURK. - lies there, chest stove in - everyone thinking "Oh poor

25

little lad" - and all the time he's dreaming of some bint.

FATHER. That'll do.

BOY. My chest... my chest don't half hurt.

FATHER. Just don't try to move, that's all.

BOY. I'm fine, no need to worry about me.

TURK. Course you're fine, it'd take more than three tons of masonry and half a church to shut you up. Ought to join a circus, lad, have fifteen woman and an elephant sit on you, lovely.

FATHER. That'll do, I said!

BOY. Where's Mum?

MOTHER. (turning nervously to face him but making no attempt to cross to him) Hallo dear. Feeling better, are you?

BOY. (regarding her) Yes.

(MRS. PRIDDY comforts DOD, wiping his face gently like a child's)

MRS. PRIDDY. There... there...

(OLD'UN and FATHER aside)

FATHER. How're we going to carry him? - there's only -

OLD'UN. He's not moving.

FATHER. What? But mister, we've got to get him to -

OLD'UN. Leave it to me, alright? I know what I'm about.

TURK. What do you mean, we're not moving him? He's got to get to a doctor and fast -

ANDY IPPS. (pointing to OLD'UN's arm) What's that?

OLD'UN. Don't you worry about that.

ANDY. You're bleeding.

26

TURK. We're not just going to sit here and let him... (he glances at THE BOY) - Hey! - (to his FATHER) He's got to get to a doctor, come on!

OLD'UN. It's OK.

ANDY. That's bad, mister, ent that arterial?

BOY. How did you do it?

OLD'UN. On the beam here. When Charlie Chaplin here throws it at me. Caught my arm.

(the above spoken simultaneously)

BOY. Beam?

ANDY. This beam was over your chest.

BOY. (simply) Oh. Is that what it was.

(There is a sudden increase of light and they all look up. / MRS. PRIDDY has found several more altar candles and is lighting them./ The tiny building fills with yellow light:/we see each person in turn as they watch, in their nightclothes, standing or sitting amidst the filth and destruction, their breath steamy in the cold, damp air, their faces dirty and scratched or bloody. /There is a sudden stillness as they watch. The dust has settled and grown damp, the fallen masonry and shattered boxpews are motionless, as though they had always been like that. /MRS. PRIDDY places the candles on fallen chunks of stone, the lectern, a man's head on a mural monument, the little communion rail. We see the place clearly for the first time.

The nave is barely ten paces by five, with enormously thick but tiny arches to the chancel and west tower, each no more than a few feet across. The floor of the tower, barely six feet square, is a foot or so lower than the nave level, and in its west wall is the main, large ceremonial door to the church, barred and bolted and very rarely used. The everyday entrance is a smaller door in the north wall.

The Georgian boxpews remain around the central aisle, now broken by beams and fallen stonework, and covered with filth. There is a huge three-decker pulpit.

The church is clustered thick with monuments and minor alterations and additions to the fabric, of all conceivable periods from early Saxon to the present, somehow crammed into the tiny space. Huge beams and buttresses shore up the

27

roof, and massive bracing irons run from wall to wall,
holding it together. The whole building is shattered and awry.

This is no "incense-church" but the tough, practical, central
building of the hamlet and its people: its air is cold and clear)

(MRS. PRIDDY finishes and stands back)

MRS. PRIDDY. (as if satisfied) There!

BOY. (simple surprise) Where are the others?

OLD'UN. They're alright.

BOY. You mean they -

OLD'UN. (heavily) I mean they're alright, that's what I mean.
They didn't come in here, they'll be miles away by now.

(PETER. I don't see how you can know that -)
(   )
(FATHER. But Mr. Williams we don't know -   ) sim.
(   )
(TURK.   How do you work that one out then?   )

(ANDY.   (shout) He said to you, didn't he?   )
(   ) sim.
(OLD'UN. (shout) They're alright, didn't you hear me? -)

(-Forcibly cutting off this train of thought and at the same
time attempting to re-establish his authority -)

- (shout) what's the matter with you, you gone deaf all of a
sudden? I said, they're alright! - probably scampering
around like a lot of hairy goats wondering what's
happened to <u>us</u> -

FATHER. But I can't see that you -

OLD'UN. (outburst) Blust, do I talk to myself? Listen! We're
not moving one step out of this old Hen (he slaps the fallen
beam with the palm of his hand) - no ifs and buts about that.
We're staying right put, oh-ho yes. You think this is the
German invasion, don't you? - you think, just because
Johnny Ipps rung the bells and we had a bomb dropped, that
the Nazis are pouring over in their millions just looking for
Old Romney here to crucify. Well listen. If they was,
you'd have had a bit more of an upset than one bang and a bit
of a shakeup. And what is there? Silence? What sort of

28

(Silence)

So the Old'un's not so silly eh? Perhaps he's not past
it after all, perhaps he's still got a point or two. Listen!
We stay here till it gets light; safest here, case they bomb
again. Now that's hard; sit tight and wait, that's hard.
It's going to take all of us, so we all sit tight, I want no
clever stuff from anyone, that clear? I know what I'm about;
and you'll do as I say.

TURK. (singing) "...and the little one said Roll over..."

(Tower end of the nave)

CHRISTINE. (whispers) We don't have to stay if we don't want.

PETER. Yea.

CHRISTINE. Who's he think he is? - not God, is he?

PETER. They all work for him, see, on this farm. Run like
a bleedin' battleship. Like kids, aren't they?

(Nave area)

MRS. PRIDDY. What about - the flooding.

OLD'UN. Eh?

MRS. PRIDDY. Well, they're going to blow up the seawall,
aren't they? - that's what they said. Flood the Marsh
here, stop the Germans landing. One hour's notice we'd
have to pack and go.

OLD'UN. I was coming to that.

TURK. Course he was.

OLD'UN. You're above the water level in this building, see?
- if they flood, you're above it. Worst that'll happen's
you'll smell a bit of damp; tragedy that, eh? They built these
old Marsh churches on little knolls of land, little bumps
raised above the sea level, just in case; the village int, but
this is. Didn't know that, did you?

29

ANDY. So you'll be alright, see.

OLD'UN. Anyhow, they'll be here before anything like that happens, rescue, oh-ho yes. Before it's light, shouldn't wonder.

ANDY. So you won't have long to wait. Soon be light now.

TURK. About six that'd be.

OLD'UN. No, gets light earlier than that now.

TURK. No it don't.

OLD'UN. About five.

TURK. Just about six I'd say.

BOY. Yea?

(Pause)

FATHER. (hesitantly) What about the boy?

ANDY. (immediately) You heard what he said.

FATHER. He needs a doctor.

(Silence)

I'm sorry Mr. Williams, but I can't just wait here and...

(They look at him)

I'm responsible. I'll go under my own risk.

OLD'UN. We'll wait till light.

FATHER. I'm sorry mister, but he's hurt. I'll get on the Fordson and drive like buggery to get someone to him. Waiting for light won't make him no better.

TURK. That's right Dad -

FATHER. (savagely) Shut it!

BOY. I'll be OK.

FATHER. No, you won't, you won't be OK, son, I won't risk it.

(Pause)

ANDY. Perhaps you didn't hear what he said.

FATHER. I - don't mean no disrispeck.

OLD'UN. Think I don't know what I'm on about then?

TURK. (aggressively) Well, it was the signal, wasn't it? - what they said? - "In the event of the Invasion, church bells will be rung" - and the Coastguard hooter - what else could it have been at 3 in the morning?

PETER. Why's it gone so quiet then?

(Pause)

MRS. PRIDDY. Where is Johnny Ipps?

MOTHER. No-one seen him?

ANDY. Last I saw was about midnight, was going to bed.

TURK. For God's sake what was he ringing for then, eh? Someone must have told him, he ent got second sight! Must have had some sort of message -

DOD. Perhaps he likes the noise.

(They all look at DOD in some surprise: he is sitting apart from them)

MRS. PRIDDY. How could he reckon the Jerries were coming?

ANDY. You know John Ipps. He's that jumpy. Hear a duck quack he'd jump over his tractor wi' fright.

BOY. (laughs)!

OLD'UN. Shut up.

ANDY. - probably just got a scare.

MRS. PRIDDY. No-one seen him?

(Silence)

FATHER. Right. I - er - I'll get moving then. Shouldn't take more than an hour, soon get someone.

OLD'UN. (looks at him)

FATHER. (pleading) He's hurt, Mr. Williams, I int got no choice, can't sit around and see him just -

TURK. (incredulous) You don't have to apologise to him for -

FATHER. (explosion) You keep out o' this, I don't need your help! You caused enough harm since... worst day of my life when you come home again!

TURK. I did what?

FATHER. You're nothing to do with me, understand? - just keep out of my way!

TURK. But I'm agreeing with you for Gods sake! - me and Mum will stay with him, and you go and get -

MOTHER. I'm going too.

(Pause)

TURK. (turning away) Ha!

MOTHER. Mrs. Priddy'll look after the boy, won't you Mrs. Priddy? And Turk. Nothing I can do, is there? - much better come with you and help, you're sure to need help -

OLD'UN. Anyone else?

MOTHER. - well, won't he, Mr. Williams, I ask you?

(Pause. They all look at her)

FATHER. (dully) There's no room.

MOTHER. I'll hold on the back, don't you worry about me - I can hold on the back like we did as kids, arms round your middle, you know?

(Silence)

TURK. (shout) Well go on then!

FATHER. Yes, well, but...

32

(They stand indecisive. OLD'UN watches them)

OLD'UN. Yea?

BOY. (sudden pain) Ah!

MRS. PRIDDY. All right, bird, don't move, try and lie still, there now.

BOY. (whimpers)

TURK. He alright?

MRS. PRIDDY. Tried to sit up, I think, must have done something.

ANDY. Try not to move, son.

BOY. Alright, Mr. Ipps, I won't. Ey - Johnny Ipps never really done that, did he?

ANDY. What?

BOY. Jump over his tractor with fright.

ANDY. P'raps not.

BOY. I'd like to have seen that. He's a very unconventional man, sometimes, isn't he, very unconventional is Johnny Ipps.

(The tractor roars into life outside. OLD'UN swings round unbelievingly. THE BOY's two parents have gone./ ANDY IPPS runs out. He can be heard shouting: they shout back.)

(Tower area)

PETER. Hey - we could do alright out of this.

CHRISTINE. What?

PETER. Compensation. If our cottage got hit or anything, they got to pay us. It's a new law.

CHRISTINE. But we only rent it.

PETER. Yea. (pause) Well - (aggressively) I shouldn't think that'd make no difference!

33

(The tractor is heard to move off and away in the darkness. We see each in turn as the sound recedes)

TURK. (bitter) Get them.

(ANDY returns and stands in the doorway)

ANDY. I couldn't do nothing.

(DOD IPPS is squatting in the chancel, next to a candle, a torn and dirty jacket over his knees. He lets out a long falling sigh as the tractor gets fainter in the distance)

DOD. Highee...eee........

(Silence. Closeup of OLD'UN, incredulous)

OLD'UN. (suddenly) Don't touch that!

TURK. Why not?

(TURK is about to pull a beamend off a pew, to clear a space for himself)

OLD'UN. Because I say not, that's why not. You could bring down the rest of the wall if you - (TURK sneers openly: OLD'UN erupts) And I'll take no lip from you! It's a waste of time trying it on with me son, you're a non-runner, you haven't got a chance, not a chance! I know you, I know about you, chick, just out to make trouble, that's your game. But I've got through more like you than you're had hot dinners. Don't they teach you no discipline in the Army nowadays? - call yourself a soldier - why aren't you fighting, eh? Strikes me as very odd you getting leave all of a sudden just when the real fighting starts,   come back home here Smart Alecking about the place, sticking in your spikes where... We don't want you back! Listen! - I'll break in time, I'll crack apart I know; but not yet, chick, oh-ho no, sweetheart, not so easy! (a movement from TURK) Don't touch that b -

(TURK calmly gives the beam a sharp tug and it comes cleanly away from the wall with no debris or dust whatsoever. He smiles at the OLD'UN)

(Tower area)

PETER. Got no rights over us. They're nutters.

34

(Nave area. MRS. PRIDDY, who has been watching
OLD'UN, turns back to THE BOY. / ANDY IPPS turns away to
the window; he says nothing./ DOD IPPS crosses to the
OLD'UN who is standing motionless, still staring at TURK)

DOD. This is John's coat.

(Pause)

John's coat, this is, my brother's. I found it.

OLD'UN. Mm? (he touches it without looking at it) Coat eh?

DOD. Yes. I found it up there, see.

OLD'UN. Uh. (deep breath: he snaps back to normal) Right
then. You're alright yourself, aren't you?

DOD. Oh yes, Mr. Williams, thank you.

OLD'UN. Right then.

(MRS. PRIDDY sings quietly to THE BOY, a child's sleeping
song. She strokes his forehead)

OLD'UN. (crossing to ANDY IPPS) Watch the boy and that woman.
Get him anything he wants. Tell me if he gets worse.

ANDY. Right, Mr. Williams.

OLD'UN. (crossing away) And don't let him move.

(Pause)

ANDY. How long till light mister?

OLD'UN. (looking at watch) My watch's broken.

ANDY. Oh? It's ticking.

OLD'UN. Yes? (holds it to ear) Mmm. The face's gone though.
Anyone else got one?

ANDY. (to all) Anyone got the time?

PETER. Time we wasn't here, daddy, time we wasn't here.

(MRS. PRIDDY sings quietly. THE BOY is almost asleep./

CHRISTINE turns restlessly onto her back: PETER, next to her, blows out the candle by her head and squats there in the shadow, watching the OLD'UN./ DOD wanders back to the chancel. He sits and lets out a long deep sigh)

DOD. Higheee...eeee...

(THE BOY has a fit of coughing. MRS. PRIDDY comforts him. He leans back. She picks up a candle and leans forward carefully to look at him./ANDY IPPS stares motionless out of a tiny Saxon window. DOD is by his feet, the torn coat in his arms./ Pan round to the OLD'UN, sitting halfway up the shattered threedecker pulpit, dominating the tiny church: his head is forward, and he fumblingly improvises a tourniquet on his bloody arm./ TURK, leaning against a wall, watches him, tossing a pebble up and down in his hand, weighing him up. The watch ticks. Fade)

(Fade up. The fractured roof of the church. A wet grey dawn sky shows through the broken beamends./ Pan down a huge crack to TURK drawing obscene drawings on the walls with charcoal. In the nave the candles are still alight./ Long pause. TURK's is the only movement)

BOY. (suddenly) Better here than outside, anyway.

(Pause. ANDY IPPS glances up at the OLD'UN; then gets up and starts to walk about restlessly)

MRS. PRIDDY. Why?

BOY. Eh?

MRS. PRIDDY. Why's it better in here?

BOY. Sheltered.

MRS. PRIDDY. Ah.

(Pause. DOD IPPS clucks his tongue. OLD'UN sits apart from the rest, facing away from them, running his finger down a crack in the stone wall)

BOY. Saturday today.

MRS. PRIDDY. Yes.

BOY. Saturn's Day.

MRS. PRIDDY. Know what my job is Saturdays?

BOY. Mm?

MRS. PRIDDY. Clean the church, here, and do the flowers, ready for Sundays.

BOY. Oh yes? (he looks round at the destruction) Got quite a job on, haven't you?

MRS. PRIDDY. Oh (laughs) I shan't do it today, no, I shan't try today!

DOD. (not looking up) Left the thresher out last night.

TURK. Oh?

DOD. Shouldn't have done that.

TURK. (disapproving) Ts ts ts ts.

DOD. Might get pinched.

TURK. Threshing machine?

DOD. Yea.

TURK. What would anyone want to pinch a threshing machine for?

DOD. (looking up) Threshing.

MRS. PRIDDY. You don't polish the brasses, you know.

BOY. No?

MRS. PRIDDY. You leave them dark. Most people polish them, but you shouldn't.

BOY. What, them vases and things?

MRS. PRIDDY. No, - the people, figures, you know -

(She scrapes some rubble away: a sixteenth century brass is revealed)

37

BOY. Oh yes.

MRS. PRIDDY. It's a man, look, and his wife, on a little hill.

BOY. What's that say?

MRS. PRIDDY. Oh I can't read that, you'd need a professor or something to tell you what that says. It's an Ipps, though, I know that.

BOY. What, like...? (he gestures to ANDY and DOD IPPS)

MRS. PRIDDY. Yes.

BOY. (impressed) Gee! Hey - Mr. Ipps did you know you had ancestors?

ANDY. We been around a long time, you know.

BOY. What relation would he be?

ANDY. I dunno. Great-great-great-great something.

BOY. Don't look too happy, do he?

MRS. PRIDDY. It's very old.

ANDY. You comfortable?

BOY. Yes. Ta.

TURK. I'm watching him, Andy, don't you fret.

ANDY. (ignoring him) Can I get you anything?

BOY. Like what?

ANDY. Well...anything?

BOY. No thanks.

ANDY. Right.

BOY. Almost light now, isn't it?

ANDY. Yeap.

BOY. Well...er (glances at the OLD'UN) - what's going to

happen?

ANDY. (heartily) Don't you worry, he knows exactly what he's about, just you wait and see!

(OLD'UN is muttering to himself: he sits crouched, his back to them, laying his fist against the chancel step, raising it and letting it fall again, like a steam hammer./ TURK draws laboriously, whistling under his breath)

BOY. Want more light Turk?

TURK. What for?

BOY. See what you're playing at.

TURK. I'm creating. Art, that's what this is, Art, boy.

BOY. I think it stinks.

TURK. Well, it's High Art. Wait till we get out of here, I'll make a fortune with people coming to see this stuff. Half-a-crown a time, turnstiles, nice little bar - the lot. Modern Church Art, see? Solve the problem of declining church attendance overnight. All we'd need then is the Old'un here to dress up in a church nightie with a mitre round his old hows-yer-fathers to bless it all, and we'd be in, lad.

ANDY. Look, why don't you belt up?

TURK. Because I'm full of the joys of life, my old teacosy, just a little ray of sunshine that's me.

BOY. Hey - do you think we'll get our names in the papers?

TURK. Right across the front page boy. It'll burst like a thunderbolt across the Romney and Walland Marsh Weekly Agricultural Gazette and Advertiser. You'll be famous, that's what. You'll be a hero. Beautiful women'll be lying down in the streets for you to walk over them -

BOY. Ehay! And I only left school four weeks.

TURK. Fantastic!

BOY. Ay. I bet I'm the first bloke from our school to have his chest bashed in in an invasion, ever!

TURK. Doddy Ipps, my little chatterbox, what would you prescribe for an agricultural apprentice with a bashed-in chest?

DOD. (nervously) Me - I dunno.

TURK. Come on now, cheer up, think of something - cup of tea, aspirin, cut his leg off?

DOD. (turning away) I don't know, see, leave me alone.

TURK. (sings as he turns back to draw) "Oh take me to your arms, Cathleen..."

(Silence. TURK draws. ANDY IPPS walks about restlessly. He suddenly stops)

ANDY. Where're them two?

TURK. What?

ANDY. That young couple there, where are they?

(They all look up at the tower area: it is empty)

DOD. Eh.

TURK. Well, run me down.

(ANDY strides to the door and out: OLD'UN and TURK follow)

TURK. (going) Hey presto, the disappearing twins.

MRS. PRIDDY. You seen them go, Dodsy?

DOD. I int seen nothing.

*(Outside the door, OLD'UN, TURK and ANDY stare at the hamlet. It is just light, but a mist has gathered and the houses are seen only as black shapes. There is an extraordinary stillness. No-one is in sight)

TURK. Ha!

ANDY. Who do they think they are?

OLD'UN. (close whisper) I didn't want them. I didn't care for
40

them.

TURK. They got their heads screwed on, anyrate.

*(Inside the church)

MRS. PRIDDY. They shouldn't have done that.

BOY. Why not?

MRS. PRIDDY. Well, it's not right, is it? We got to stick
together!

*(Outside the church)

OLD'UN. If they're there, bring them back. Don't argue with
them, and be fast.

ANDY. Right mister. (he goes)

TURK. You see them go?

OLD'UN. No.

TURK. They'll be there by now though, won't they? - they'll
be laughing.

*(Inside the church)

DOD. She's going to have a baby.

MRS. PRIDDY. Only been here four months. He works in some
munitions factory in Ashford, cycles there every day. Near
twelve miles that'd be. Stupid thing to do, innit?

*(ANDY IPPS walking in the mist. His feet suddenly splash
and he stops, surprised. Water stretches ahead of him,
several inches deep, quite still: it surrounds the houses,
looming black shapes around him)

ANDY. (shouts) Anyone at home?

(Silence. He shivers)

*(Outside the church)

TURK. And the boy's bad, there's blood on his cough. (no
reply: he starts to explode) Look -

OLD'UN. I know what I'm doing. Just do what I say, that's
all any of you have to do.

TURK. So what do we do? Just hang about?

(OLD'UN. Leave all that to me -   )
(   ) overlapping
(TURK. - oh that'd suit you fine, wouldn't it -   )
(   )
(OLD'UN. - you'll be looked after, don't you worry -   )
(   )
(TURK. - I'm king of the castle, don't tell me anything -)

OLD'UN. (topping) Why don't you go then? What's stopping you?
- that's the road. Go on, why don't you push off?

TURK. I'm not leaving him.

OLD'UN. (cynical) Oh yes, yes.

TURK. Anyhow, I might get caught halfway. You know, if they
blow up the seawall -

OLD'UN. (grunts)

TURK. Well, no point in asking for it - we don't know, do we?

OLD'UN. I know.

TURK. Course you do. You know every bloody thing, don't you?
- why no-one's come yet, what's happening -

OLD'UN. (immovable) They'll come.

  *(Inside the church)

MRS. PRIDDY. He knows what he's up to.

BOY. Well, what?

MRS. PRIDDY. Oh I don't know, he hasn't told me!

42

BOY. Well, why don't you ask then?

MRS. PRIDDY. (shocked) Oh no! - you got to <u>trust</u> him!

(Pause)

BOY. Has he always been like this?

MRS. PRIDDY. Like what?

BOY. Well...

DOD. I seen him sit by himself, like - head down - dinnertimes, and talk - you know, to himself.

BOY. I don't think he's very interested in us. I mean - <u>us</u>. You know - as <u>people</u>.

MRS. PRIDDY. Well - (explanation) - he's in charge.

*(Outside the church)

TURK. And there's this. You reckon all these old churches were built above waterlevel?

OLD'UN. All the Marsh churches -

TURK. Yea, alright, alright. So: - How do you know they haven't sunk, subsided, you know.

OLD'UN. Eh?

TURK. Well, look at it, it's bloody falling apart, and it's sunk, maybe feet - look - all this Marshy soil, it's keeling over. So how do you know it's still above water level?

```
(OLD'UN. (beat) Don't you worry, I know all about that - )  o
(                                                          )  v
(TURK. Oh you do? Well what the -                          )  e
(                                                          )  r
(OLD'UN. -We'll wait an hour.                              )  l
```
(overlapping)

(Pause)

TURK. We'll what?

OLD'UN. (bluster) Now look -

43

(TURK. You know something? I don't think you've   )
(got an idea in your head!   )
(   )
(OLD'UN. Got to stick here -   )
(   )
(TURK. You're just...trying to hold it together somehow,)
(waiting for... (he shakes his head)... I don't know! A)
(bloody miracle or...   )
(   )
(OLD'UN. - only thing that makes sense -   )
(   )
(TURK. Why don't you say? Why don't you tell them   )
(you don't know, so we can at least talk about -   )
(   )
(OLD'UN. You leave it all to me -   )
(   )
(TURK. Oh, you know it all, don't you - right then,   )
(bloody do something about it!   )

overlapping

OLD'UN. (slamming hard back) Yes - that's just it - do something, anything, doesn't matter what, does it? - anything
   so long as you don't have to think - eh? What would you do?
   Throw the boy over your shoulder and start running? -

TURK. Well at least -

OLD'UN. - he'd be dead before you got a mile. Send someone
   else for help? What if they blow the walls?

TURK.   OK, so what are we going to do?

OLD'UN. (in the same tone as all the other times) You leave
   all that to me, boy, I know what's what.

   (He turns to re-enter the church)

TURK. (shouting after him) God'll have to watch out with you
   around, won't he? - or he'll find himself out of a job!

   *(Inside the church, as OLD'UN comes in)

DOD. He's got different, your brother.

BOY. Yea?

DOD. - since he's been away. He never used to carry on like
   this.

44

MRS. PRIDDY. Used to be a serious lad; bit mad sometimes, mind you, but - serious.

BOY. He is now.

MRS. PRIDDY. Oh no, he's not, he's not, what do you mean?

TURK. (entering) How's me little angelface brother then? Playing leapfrog yet?

BOY. Not so bad, how's yourself?

TURK. You keep your hands off Mrs. Priddy, you randy beast, I've got her marked out for meself the long winter evenings.

BOY. Where's Mum and Dad got to, you reckon?

TURK. What do you think, Mrs. P?

BOY. Should be back by now, shouldn't they? Shouldn't take that long. 'Bout time someone came.

TURK. Just been talking about that, haven't we Mr. Williams? -

(He catches OLD'UN's eye, and hesitates. He looks at MRS. PRIDDY and DOD, who are watching him)

MRS. PRIDDY. (almost under her breath) If it's something unpleasant, we'd rather not know.

(Pause)

TURK. (shout) But you got -

DOD. You got a plan then?

TURK. Eh?

DOD. You got a plan?

TURK. (beat) That's not the point -

OLD'UN. Isn't it?

(TURK stares at him: then turns abruptly to stare at the others. He starts to learn./ He turns abruptly, angrily, and stares out of a window. The others wait. Silence)

BOY. Don't often see you with people, Dodsy.

DOD. No, I don't see many people.

BOY. Why's that then?

DOD. Oh...I don't know.

BOY. What you staying over there for?

(DOD crosses into THE BOY, nervously. He squats down beside him)

DOD. I know a good doctor.

BOY. I don't think I've ever seen you this close before.

DOD. He'd put you right.

BOY. Oh yea?

DOD. He looks after me. You know what he says? I'm all rotten inside.

BOY. You're what?

DOD. Rotten - all me innerds, going soft. He's a good doctor, I like him.

BOY. Sounds terrific.

DOD . There's this little thing, see, like a little worm, or grub, like a little tiny germ.

BOY. (screws up his face) What - eating you?

DOD. Oh no, nothing like that. No. (pause)

BOY. What then?

DOD. Well - just - lives there, these little worms (indicates his abdomen and laughs) Always been there.

BOY. Can't they do anything about it?

DOD. What do you mean?

BOY. Well - can't he treat you? - give you something for it?

46

DOD. Oh no. It's me, isn't it? I mean... (he searches) ...It's
   me!

OLD'UN. (suddenly) Listen!

   (Silence)

   (TURK launches into unnatural vigour and din)

(TURK. "And the waters as they flow, seem to whisper...")
(   )
((OLD'UN. That'll do, I'm trying to -   )   ) overlapping
((   ) sim.   )
((MRS. PRIDDY. Please Turk don't make -))   )
(   )
(TURK. What's up with you, don't you know a trained   )
(voice when you hear one?   )
(   )
(OLD'UN. Just shut it boy -   )

TURK. Remember me in the choir here, I used to sing in the
   choir, didn't I Mrs. Priddy? Lovely voice I had,
   beautiful.

MRS. PRIDDY. Loud, anyrate.

BOY. I didn't know you was in the choir Turk?

TURK. Didn't Mum and Dad tell you nothing about me? I'd
   sing you psalms by the square mile, son, rattle off the
   responses that fast you couldn't tell one word from another.
   See that mark, that burn there? - where I stubbed out me
   ciggies, worked up to a packet of twenty per service.

BOY. (chuckling) Go on, you'd be seen!

TURK. Ah, I used to blow the smoke into a little hole, where is
   it? - there, see, there look. Into that bloke's tomb, see?
   Had a cigar one Christmas, blew the smoke in, heard him
   coughing. S'true, honest! Wouldn't think I was the choirboy
   type, would you? - don't seem possible now.

OLD'UN. (grunts, amused)

TURK. Feels funny, this bench, I can't... (he is trying to get
   comfortable in his old choirstall) Still, that's gone now
   though, that's the past, I got out of all that.

MRS. PRIDDY. Why the Army though?

TURK. Eh?

MRS. PRIDDY. What you go in the Army for? - you of all people.

TURK. Action, I thought, excitement, not rot away down here like you lot; join the Army and see the world, you know.

MRS. PRIDDY. And did you?

TURK. Three years Aldershot, four years Catterick, very exotic; only action I saw in seven years was chucking-out time at The Volunteer.

BOY. Been in London through the Blitz though, haven't you?

TURK. I have love, I wasn't counting that. Right good time was that.

BOY. Fun, is it?

TURK. What? It's been the time of my life, son. Everything on fire, you know, houses and factories. A great roaring orgy. You can breathe in that lot. I'm learning more from the blitz than in my whole seven years service and that's saying something. It's a bloody good time, son, don't let anyone tell you different. When we get out of this lot, we'll have you right out too, little brother mine. I mean, right out. Of all this... (gesture)... crippling, stifling...

(OLD'UN leans forward pointedly)

OLD'UN. Got something to put in its place then?

MRS. PRIDDY. My mother was killed in the Zeppelin raid, the Great War, you know, when they bombed around here. We didn't know about airraids then.

TURK. Doing a lot of good, the Blitz is. Making people stand on their own two feet. Getting rid of things that'd been there too long, eh Mr. Williams? - what do you say Mr. Williams? - letting in some fresh air! - so's you can breathe!

DOD. Andy.

(They turn. ANDY IPPS enters and sits quietly)

48

OLD'UN. Well?

ANDY. Well - old Bob Traffords had it, then.

MRS. PRIDDY. No.

ANDY. And his ol' woman, shouldn't be surprised. There int nothing left of their house, just a pile of bricks and stuff, I reckon she's under that lot. But you can see him, he's only part covered, poor mannie. Must have happened, quick, though, thank the good Lord, instantaneous, I'd say. All the other houses is alright, 'cept for broken windows and things, I went through them all; there's no-one.

(Silence)

BOY. They've all gone then.

ANDY. Yeap.

MRS. PRIDDY. Well I'll go to 'ell.

OLD'UN. You're sure he's...

ANDY. Yeap. He's dead right enough.

OLD'UN. Ah.

TURK. Old Bob Trafford.

OLD'UN. (grunts)

ANDY. They was good old sticks, weren't they Mr. Williams?

MRS. PRIDDY. Poor old man. They was gentle, wasn't they? A gentle old pair. Wouldn't say boo to a goose. Well, I'll go to 'ell. Don't seem possible, do it.

OLD'UN. She were an Upton, warn't she, from out Snargit?

MRS. PRIDDY. I mind they took in ol' Jacky Forge one winter, him what used to live out Walland Marsh in a little kennel thing.

ANDY. Didn't get no thanks, did they?

MRS. PRIDDY. No, that they didn't, no, not from him!

(Pause. OLD'UN is muttering to himself)

BOY. What... did he look like?

ANDY. How do you mean?

BOY. Mr. Trafford, you know, did he look... well - (he gestures)

ANDY. He looked dead, son.

MRS. PRIDDY. Could you tell what had happened?

ANDY. (shakes head) 'Twas only his shoulders and head sticking out of all the rubble, all wet, near plastering wet. It's nearly under water too.

TURK. Water?

ANDY. Yes, nearly up to the church here. No more than a foot deep down there, though, and not rising or moving or anything - I reckon one of them bombs must have breached the dyke a bit, but they stopped it up now.

OLD'UN. (grunts)

(Pause)

ANDY. You know all them old brown photos they had on their walls? - all their old aunties and grandfathers and great uncles and such? - well, they're scattered all around him, on the rubble, wet and torn and screwed up, all over the place. Some of them was in the water, just floating away. And you know what I thought? - there's no-one left now that'd know who all them people were. There int, is there? Like they was...fading. (pause) I brought some food. Cheese and stuff.

(He puts down a cardboard box)

There int much.

(Pause. Very faintly the water can be heard lapping outside. OLD'UN mutters)

MRS. PRIDDY. Queer old things, the years.

(Silence)

DOD. (quietly) Look!

50

BOY. What?

DOD. Up there! Look at that!

(They look up. Plaster has fallen away from the top of a
wall, revealing a small part of a mediaeval wall painting.
It is crowded with faces, impassively staring out and down
at the beholder, part of a Last Judgment)

TURK. Gee.

BOY. What is it?

MRS. PRIDDY. All them faces.

ANDY. It's a painting, innit? - an old painting.

BOY. It must have been under that plaster that's broke off.
Think there's more of it?

ANDY. Clever, innit?

BOY. Bit better than your efforts, Turk.

TURK. Yea?

ANDY. There's a bit more just coming away - see - here it
comes - ha! -

(TURK shies a stone: a further piece of plaster falls away,
revealing a more striking face)

DOD. Higheeee!

(Silence. They are awed)

TURK. (without his usual swashbuckling conviction) Not a very
sexy lot are they? Look like mediaeval NCOs.

(It falls flat. Silence./There is a distant sound, like a long,
deep boom carried on the wind from a long way off, and
muffled by the mist. A trickle of sand falls from the roof
in a thin line)

BOY. That's them, innit? That's them on the seawall.

TURK. (grimly) Well. We'll soon know how we're fixed now.

(The speed picks up)

51

BOY. What you get to eat?

TURK. Don't move, I'll get it.

BOY. - in the box there.

TURK. Bashed about a bit, innit? What you bring then?

> (He tips it out onto an altar tomb. Out fall dry earth, two soggy sandwiches, half a loaf, a chunk of cheese and some raw potatoes)

> Oh Mr. Ipps, you're such an elegant host. Good bit of Romney Marsh in these, int there? (holds them up to the light) Bit heavy on the loam, int they? Who's hungry then. What about you, Einstein? (to DOD)

DOD. What's in them?

BOY. Cheese and grit or tomato and grit.

DOD. You're joking.

TURK. Eh?

DOD. Int he joking?

BOY. That's right.

DOD. Ah ha. (and he fixes TURK with a slight glint in his eye)

MRS. PRIDDY. Mr. Williams.

OLD'UN. (looks up)

MRS. PRIDDY. Can I go to my house for - you know?

OLD'UN. Eh?

MRS. PRIDDY. I want to spend a penny, is it alright if I -

OLD'UN. No, stay inside. Your house is alright.

MRS. PRIDDY. I thought as Mr. Ipps had -

OLD'UN. Round there, by the pulpit, against the wall.

MRS. PRIDDY. I don't think I... oh...

(Embarrassed, she crosses up to a tiny box pew by the
pulpit. After a blushing look round, she squats: her head
protrudes)

OLD'UN. Think I was born yesterday.

TURK. Why shouldn't she want to see her house's OK for God's
sake - it's pretty natural, isn't it?

OLD'UN. (reddening) Don't you shout at me, boy -

TURK. Supposed to switch herself off is she? - pretend she
doesn't care? (shouts and bangs on the pew MRS. PRIDDY is
in) Don't you take no notice of him, love, you do just what
you want!

(MRS. PRIDDY turns from pink to scarlet. Cut to OLD'UN,
muttering to himself as he tries to loosen the tourniquet on
his arm. He gives it a wrench with exasperation and
winces with the pain)

BOY. You alright Mr. Williams? Can I help?

OLD'UN. (crossing to him) Here - cut this.

BOY. Cut it?

OLD'UN. Or untie it or something. (he produces an old penknife)

BOY. (cutting) There.

OLD'UN. (grunts)

(ANDY IPPS watches./OLD'UN sits and rips a strip from
JOHNNY IPPS' coat on the floor, and starts rebandaging./
It is full daylight now)

BOY. Will it be alright like that Mr. Williams?

(OLD'UN does not reply, concentrating on the bandaging.
Quick pan up to THE BOY's face: we see him lift his eyes
from the OLD'UN's arm to his face, and look at it./DOD is
sitting on the edge of a pew, rocking back and forth, eyes
flickering over at the OLD'UN./ANDY turns away to the
window, and looks out./We see his point of view: the water
has crept up to within a few feet of the church. The fog hangs
heavier.

ANDY pauses, alarmed: then launches in, cheerfully, to THE

BOY, distracting him)

ANDY. This is where I used to sit, this pew, I was your age.
There's my initials, see? Took me a whole Lent to cut
them, 1907 or 8 that'd be.

BOY. Did no-one stop you?

ANDY. Well, folk can't see in these high old pews, if you sat
on the floor, see. All sorts of things used to go on,
dint they mister? Old Mrs. Stanley conceived six times in
here, during Psalm 119; each year, nineteenth Sunday after
Trinity, regular as clockwork.

(MRS. PRIDDY, still squatting, mumbles something and
flaps her hand. TURK tears out several pages from a
hymnbook and passes them to her)

Jim Stanley, her husband, he got killed at the Somme; and
come the nineteenth after Trinity for years after, she'd get
in a terrible stage. Old Mr. Wright the sidesman wouldn't
go near her to take the collection, said he valued his honour.
She got him, though, 1919; they had to repeat five verses of
"Come forth, oh fiery Habakkuk" before he got out of her
pew. He had to retire after that, cos he started to shake
so much taking the collection he'd set up a loud jingling folk
didn't care for; come the nineteenth after Trinity it used to
get fair deafening. (pause) That was Jim Stanley that was,
her husband, was in my regiment.

TURK. I didn't know you was in the Army, Andy!

ANDY. Buffs, I was in. Sergeant.

TURK. Well well.

ANDY. Royal East Kents. 'Long with my mates there.

(He nods at a small wooden board on the wall, painted
in an amateur fashion: "The Great War: A. Beeching, A.
Grocett, H. Massey, J. Stanley. 'The last enemy that shall
be destroyed is death'")

I loved it. Like to have stayed.

BOY. Why didn't you?

ANDY. Invalided out.

TURK. Oh?

ANDY. (indicating his chest) Gas. That was when all them went. (nods at the board again)

OLD'UN. Drowned.

BOY. Was they?

OLD'UN. That's what gas does to your lungs, drowns you; they was drowned.

(Pause. The water laps outside. TURK watches and listens to them)

ANDY. That was the pew, look, that old Mrs. Stanley had. You look and you'll see the scorch marks she and old Mr. Wright made on the floor that morning.

MRS. PRIDDY. (rejoining them) I used to sit over here, this pew, I was a girl. Square, see, so we all faced each other, and when we knelt our noses touched!

BOY. (weak smile) Oh yea?

MRS. PRIDDY. Everyone used to come to church then, you know, three times on a Sunday, from all the farms around here, everyone.

BOY. That's a lot of praying.

ANDY. Ah-ha, it was, it was!

MRS. PRIDDY. We used to feel very holy and righteous Sunday night, didn't we Mr. Williams?

OLD'UN. (grunts)!

ANDY. Remember your father reading the lessons, mister? -

OLD'UN. (to THE BOY) Farm foreman, then -

ANDY. - bellow it, rather! Bit of an actor, wasn't he?

MRS. PRIDDY. Mighty pair of lungs he had. Even you used to laugh!

(ANDY. Or a bishop, should have been a bishop!)
(   ) sim.
(OLD'UN. (chuckles)!   )

MRS. PRIDDY. We used to say he made the Sermon on the Mount
    sound like Hiawatha; give him the Book of Job and he'd
    throw cattle into fits eight miles off. (to THE BOY) Everyone
    had his own pew then, you know. Mr. Hart, that's Mr.
    Hart's father that owned the farm, he sat there, very
    dignified. The Ippses sat there, that bench, bare knees and
    all -

ANDY. Thirteen of us, one time! - and my cousins - Doddy here
    ...

MRS. PRIDDY. We used to come in early, we three sisters, and
    watch for everyone else to arrive. Best part of the week that
    was. The Terrys was always next after us, then the Stanleys,
    here comes the Finns, here's the Bayleys...

OLD'UN. Mr. Hart was always last in and first out and never
    gave less than gold.

MRS. PRIDDY... everyone in order, everyone in his place. Lot
    to be said for that, you know. It was calm and dignified.
    Gracious, that's what it was. Mind you, lot of hypocrites,
    some of them, but there it all was - order, happiness.

    (Pause: TURK watches and listens)

    We had a choir then, mostly cowmen, and my goodness they
    sounded like it sometimes; I've known visiting clergymen be
    terrified out of their wits when they started "Arise ye Gates
    of Canaan". We used to raise the roof on them old hymns,
    melt the lead on the roof, that's what my old dad used to say!

    (ANDY and OLD'UN laugh)

    Oh, I suppose it all seems very silly, now, and old hat
    and... simple. But, do you know, I really think people
    were happier. Yes, I do. Yes, I really think so. Course,
    that's all dead and gone now, together with nearly everyone
    that knew it -

ANDY. - and there was some very peculiar people among them,
    wasn't there, when you come to think!

 MRS. PRIDDY. (laughing) Oh, I don't know, I don't know!

56

OLD'UN. (smiles)

(Pause)

MRS. PRIDDY. Look at the old place now, eh? Doesn't seem
possible. It don't.

OLD'UN. (smacks his lips) No.

ANDY. Remember that old rhyme we had at school? - 'bout
the people?

MRS. PRIDDY. Oh yes!

ANDY. Yes - er - started with the shops, didn't it?

MRS. PRIDDY. "Mrs. Butler, dealer in stamps" -

(OLD'UN. That's it!)
(   ) simultaneously
(ANDY. You got it!   )

MRS. PRIDDY. - that was the old Post Office - "Over the road
they take in tramps"

OLD'UN. Beehive.

MRS. PRIDDY. That was the old Beehive, the pub, remember the
old Beehive, next to Mrs. Nobles? (she recites with
childish sing-song emphasis on the beat; ANDY and OLD'UN
mouth the words:)

"Mrs. Butler, dealer in stamps,
Over the road they take in tramps.
Jimmy Jordan, good shoemaker -"

Then what was it?

(During the following scene, they recall this rhyme among
themselves, in the background, repeating phrases, searching
their memories, sometimes reciting in unison. It lists in
childish fashion all the long-dead inhabitants of pre-1914 Old
Romney:*

---

*See page 98.

It is the happiest we shall see these old people:
destruction surrounds them, fallen roof, shattered stone)

(TURK has crossed to the chancel and is building a little
pile of stones to knock down)

TURK. Where have they got to, then, the Brave and Bleeding
British Army? Hope they're not too long, I got a skirt.

DOD. What, tonight?

TURK. Yes.

DOD. Well, that's no good, is it?

TURK. Why not?

DOD. Well... (he struggles)...There's a War On.

TURK. But that doesn't mean I got to give it up, does it? That's
not part of the Economy Drive is it? Better not tell me
randy little brother there, or you'll have to tie him down.

DOD. (looks blank)

ANDY. (in background) "Mrs. Terry, jam and treacle," -

MRS. PRIDDY. (happily) Not Mrs. Terry, that wasn't Mrs.
Terry!

ANDY. No.

OLD'UN. (smiling) Yes it was!

    (They continue behind:)

TURK. Know the trouble with you Dodsy? You're dim.

DOD. (looks at him) Yes.

TURK. I reckon your heart's in the right place but you int got no head, have you? You ought to have more fun.

DOD. Fun?

TURK. Yea. (starts to lob stones at the target) You ought to enjoy it all more.

DOD. Oh, I have enjoyment man.

TURK. You do? What at, eh? Crochet work? Heroin?

DOD. No -

TURK. What then?

DOD. Well - see - I play the cornet.

TURK. You do?

DOD. Yea, I'm first cornet man.

TURK. Well, what do you know! That's new then! What band's that?

DOD. Army.

TURK. You what?

DOD. Salvation Army.

TURK. (is speechless)

DOD. Over Romney. I'm not very religious.

TURK. Well, roll on! Getaway! How many in the band?

DOD. Five.

TURK. Oh.

(The rhyme continues, sing-song, in the background)

DOD. We're not very good, you know, but... I like it.

TURK. Sure.

BOY. Play Sundays too sometimes, don't you Dodsy?

TURK. In the streets?

BOY. Yea. They march too.

TURK. What, in uniform?

DOD. Bits.

BOY. Bits of uniform.

TURK. What, braid, peak cap and all that?

DOD. Bits.

TURK. I must come and see this.

(TURK resumes lobbing. DOD joins in)

DOD. You'd be the only one then; we're not very good.

BOY. Old Mrs. Godfray once give them five shillings to play
outside Mrs. Martin's house; and she give them seven-
and-six to go back and play outside Mrs. Godfray's.

TURK. What did you do?

DOD. Ha!

BOY. They kept going backwards and forwards till they'd made
three pounds, took it to the Crown and had a right do.

(DOD grins)

TONY. Here, you're not so silly, are you?

(The rhyme continues: OLD'UN, MRS. PRIDDY and ANDY
are seen muzzy in the background, sitting in a little circle,
swaying in and out like opera singers as they rack their
brains and then triumphantly producing several phrases,
sometimes overlapping, like a canon or fugue./ THE BOY
mimes playing a passage on the cornet: he sways and blows)

DOD. You play, Turk?

TURK. No-o-o, mate. Wish I did though.

60

DOD. It's good, you know? You sort of blow... and play and that, and...

TURK. (smiling) Yea?

DOD. Maybe it isn't very musical, what comes out, it's a bit of a noise perhaps, but... you blow, and... oh!... (he lifts his head; his face glows)

(THE BOY lifts his imaginary cornet to blow a high note. In the background, the three old people triumphantly remember the last line in unison, and laugh gloriously. Fade)

(Fade up on OLD'UN's arm, which he is slowly re-bandaging: the large amount of blood he has lost can clearly be seen./Pan round to see the others sprawling asleep./BOY is heard coughing. Camera moves to find him and reaches him. OLD 'UN is comforting him./Coughing stops)

OLD'UN. Alright?

BOY. Yes. Thanks.

OLD'UN. Hurt?

BOY. Bit.

OLD'UN. Not long now.

BOY. Ah?

OLD'UN. They'll be here.

BOY. Something suddenly seemed to go funny - inside me - (indicates chest)

OLD'UN. (grunts)

BOY. Oh, I'm not worried about it. Funny though; felt like something... giving, starting to give.

(Pause)

BOY. How's your arm, Mr. Williams?

OLD'UN. (mutters)

61

BOY. They asleep?

(He looks at the murals: more faces are showing, and beside
them are big eighteenth century texts, painted onto the wall)

So quiet, isn't it? Absolutely still. Look at all them faces.
And them huge old texts. Like they was made of red-hot
iron, like they wanted to burn themselves into you. But -
dead quiet. 'Cept me blood...tapping away in me ears.
Usually there's something, isn't there? - train in the
distance, or just... trees, but - I can't hear nothing,
nothing at all.

(He stares at the brass)

Look at that bloke's face. That's hundreds of years old,
that is. I shouldn't be surprised if he sat in this seat here,
with his old woman. Wonder what language they spoke.

OLD'UN. English, I suppose.

BOY. They couldn't have.

OLD'UN. Why not?

BOY. What, like us?

OLD'UN. More or less.

BOY. Eh. You don't think there was ever any other time like this
except right now.

OLD'UN. Eh?

BOY. How long they been dead, do you reckon?

OLD'UN. Oh hundreds of years.

BOY. You think people like that must have been different to you
- I don't know how, but - different, not like you and me.
(pause) You know, when I was three or something, and my
grandad died, I couldn't sort of understand what had happened
to him. And somehow I thought he turned into a sort of a
ghost and hung about in church here, waiting for the Last
Judgement, with all the other dead people. And they all
sat next to each other on the old pews back there that nobody
don't use nowadays, not saying much, eating toffees out of
a paper bag.

OLD'UN. Doing what?

BOY. I know, it's mad, isn't it? - but I reckoned the angels
used to bring them all packets of toffees to keep them going
till the Latter Day. There was my Auntie Doris, with one
of them high-necked dresses like in the photo over our mantle-
piece. And my sister, who died before I was born, see, and my
little cousin Essie and uncle Bill with the big moustache and the
watch, killed in the Great War. And there they all sat
around, sort of quiet and relaxed and dignified, not saying
much - except "pass the toffees, please". And there'd
be all their friends, and the people killed in the Zeppelin raid,
and this bloke (the brass) in his armour, and all before
that, right back and back till they built this place, all
sitting around and waiting. And when my grandad come, they
all moved up one, and he sat down and had a toffee too. And
then he started smiling.

OLD'UN. Smiling?

BOY. Yes, didn't I say? They was all smiling in a funny way,
as if they had a secret, but I couldn't see what it was.

OLD'UN. And weren't they doing nothing else?

BOY. Not really. They were just sort of... themselves, all
quiet. But they did seem to be waiting for something,
listening, straining their ears for something I couldn't hear.

OLD'UN. What?

BOY. The End, I suppose. The Thunder and Lightning, the Trum-
pets and that, the Hallelujah Chorus, the Latter Day, you
know, when the Heavens will Split Right Open!

(Under the door there appears the tiniest trickle of water:
it runs silently across a flagstone, no more than a drop)

BOY. Look at that old spider. He must be wondering what it's
all about. Look at him, rushing about like mad. I suppose
we broke into his home, and he's shifting his food and
things. Look - he's got something on his back, that funny
red lump there.

OLD'UN. It's a little growth or something. He's got something
wrong with him.

BOY. (screwing up his face) Oh.

63

(Pause)

OLD'UN. When I was a chick, I used to borrow the broom from
my mother's kitchen and go sweeping the bit of grazing
behind our house for the little creeping things that lived
there. And do you know, in two minutes you'd get half
a bucket of them? - a glistening crawling heap of grass-
hoppers and beetles, and spiders and caterpillars and little
blue butterflies, and dozens of tiny creatures no bigger
than a whisker I didn't even know the name of, hundreds
and hundreds, the grass was alive with them. Now you'd
be lucky to get that many in an hour. It's these chemicals
and sprays and factory things they're starting to use -
they don't know what'll happen, they don't. People don't
think. They don't understand how it all... fits together.
And you can't avoid it, you know, every stream has got a
tiny bit of these poisons in them now, every joint and
bone, see, in every person, everything alive; you breathe
it in from the air with every breath, just a tiny bit. And
it's all starting to run down like a gigantic clock - ever so
slowly at first, mind you, and gently too, almost...
tenderly, as if Someone was afraid of hurting us. But it's
all going; the otter's going, and the eel; and little fieldmice -
I saw barely a score this harvest. And look at the weather!
- look what all these aeroplanes and flying things have done
to that! (THE BOY conceals a smile) People don't think!
It's a pattern, old as old, you just can't hack through the
middle of it! (pause) You know, sometimes, just out of
respect for all the... Magnificence of it - that used to be -
I wish it would all go up in one glorious bang - quick, and get
it over with. Like my old dad wanted for himself. You
never knew him, did you? - used to read the lesson here.

BOY. Yes, I know.

OLD'UN. He was a tough old Christian gentleman, but he never
let Christianity stand in his way if there was a job to be
done. Ran this place like a ship - tough on everyone,
most of all on himself, but they all believed in him, see.
Looked like his late Majesty King George, with his
beard, 'cept my dad was tall and bolt upright, eye like an
eagle, voice like a foghorn, by God he used to make them
jump, bit of an actor with it. But he ran it all magnificently
- everything shipshape, and fresh and brisk, everything
in its place. Well - he got hit in the Zeppelin raid, lost
his leg and had to hole up inside; got old and senile and
wetting the armchairs, you know. He tried to run things
from inside at first - sending out orders from this armchair,

but it nearly drove him mad, because he couldn't see what
was happening, and he cared so much. I don't care, son,
no, not any more; I daren't care, that's the truth of it.
But he did, and it broke his heart. Old Dr. Proctor
wouldn't let him die, kept pumping him full of stuff,
chemicals and such, to keep him like a cabbage - and he
used to weep like a child - "why won't they let me go?"
He felt an unbearable insult to... everything he'd known and
valued. There's no dignity, they should have let him blow
his brains out and have done; but no, they kept everything
sharp out of his way, he had to eat with a huge wooden spoon
thing, and they put old mackintoshes over the chairs
before he sat. He felt he was drowning, he'd weep to
me and beg me to do something, anything, get the coal
hammer and smash his head in, anything, he couldn't
bear it, this slow - petering out. And I tell you, there are
times when I want to get hold of a bloody great hammer, a
great sledgehammer, and smash it all in, smash everything
here, the lot, every window, every door, every brick to
the ground. Every tree even. Get rid of it, burn it, smash
it all to dust, out of... Respect! - for what it all has been!
Mind you, I'd break my heart afterwards, I reckon I'd cry
like a child, but I'd smash, I'd smash all the same!

TURK. (gives a curious, high, half-chuckle noise, that sighs
away on the end of his breath)

OLD'UN. Eh?

BOY. It's Turk. He's asleep.

(There is a distant sound, like a long deep boom carried on
the wind from far off, muffled by the mist. A trickle of sand
falls from the roof in a thin line, and the roof moves,
delicately./ The OLD'UN rises abruptly and faces the
body of the church. He stands staring at it, his huge arms
dangling on either side of him. The building creaks and
moves gently around him as if it were breathing. The watch
ticks)

BOY. (sharply) Listen!

(Pause. TURK wakes instantly)

TURK. I don't hear nothing.

BOY. Shush.

(Pause)

OLD'UN. What?

BOY. Dunno. Sort of... droning noise.

(Pan along row of listening faces: BOY, OLD'UN, DOD
IPPS, ANDY IPPS, MRS. PRIDDY, and lastly TURK)

TURK. (who is lying on his tum) Nothing now.

BOY. No.

ANDY. You dint imagine it, did you?

BOY. I don't think so.

OLD'UN. What did it sound like?

BOY. Like a... like a drum.

OLD'UN. A drum?

BOY. A drum. Like someone tapping on a drum.

(Pause)

TURK. I know what it is. It's the Salvation Army come to see
why Dodsy isn't at band practice.

DOD. No.

TURK. Eh?

DOD. I play the drum.

TURK. I thought you played the cornet?

DOD. I do. And the drum too, see. And the tuba sometimes.

TURK. Blimey. Proper little one-man band, aren't you? What
happens when you get a number where the cornet and the drum
are playing at the same time?

DOD. We can't play it.

TURK. Well, stroll on.

(THE BOY laughs. The laughter dies and the tension creeps back. DOD, ANDY and MRS. PRIDDY steal a glance at the OLD'UN's face. TURK swings over onto his back. OLD'UN rises and walks to the door)

BOY. Candle's getting low.

(Pause. TURK starts to whistle)

BOY. Look at them drawings. Like Ashford Public Lavs in here, isn't it?

TURK. Like what? You're a moron, you are; a cretin. These - (a magnificent gesture) - these are Masterpieces.

BOY. Yea?

TURK. But yes. Take this one now. It's entitled "A Bit of Crumpet". Comes complete with built-in toilet roll, 550 guineas, cash on the nail.

BOY. Well, you see, I want something to go in me coalhole.

TURK. Ah-ha yes, a connoisseur. What colour's your coalhole, sir?

BOY. Black.

TURK. Black, eh? What about this? It needs a man of refinement to appreciate this, sir. It's called "The Young Lady of Ealing" after the famous poem, which you will find inscribed on the back.

BOY. I'll take two.

TURK. Will I wrap them for you now sir, or will you send your lorry?

(THE BOY laughs. The laughter dies and the tension returns again. Pause)

ANDY. I can hear it now.

TURK. Yea?

OLD'UN. (grunts, meaning 'I can't')

ANDY. It's like a drum, too.

(They listen)

TURK. Is it one of ours?

(OLD'UN. Shush!)
( )   sim.
(ANDY. Quiet!)

    (Pause)

TURK. "At the third stroke, it will be -"

OLD'UN. Shut your noise.

TURK. I can't hear nothing. Bloody quiet, if you ask me.

OLD'UN. Nobody did.

TURK. All right, I can talk, can't I? I don't have to get
    permission, do I? What is this, bloody Sunday School?

BOY. There it is!

    (The sounds of an amphibious jeep can be heard approaching)

OLD'UN. I can hear it now.

MRS. PRIDDY. Yes.

BOY. You see?

ANDY. That's them, though, isn't it? That's someone coming?

    (All but THE BOY and OLD'UN crowd to the little windows
    and peer out)

  *(Outside. The mist has thickened and the houses can now
    barely be seen. The water has silently drawn right up
    to the church)

   *(Inside)

ANDY. Took their time, didn't they?

BOY. They must have got through, mustn't they? - my Mum and
    Dad?

ANDY. The Army, it'll be, from up Ashford.

68

BOY. Do you reckon they'll be with them?

MRS. PRIDDY. Could be.

OLD'UN. (triumphant) That's them, see? They're here! Have you fine, lad, there'll be a doctor. I said they'd come, didn't I?

DOD. I'm hungry.

TURK. Hallo hallo, he's off again. Can't keep the old tummy quiet, can you?

BOY. Piles of Christmas Pud they'll be sending, Dodsy, if they know you're here, and pork chops and turkey and things; just to keep you going.

TURK. You're catching on lad, aren't you?

ANDY. Funny noise, innit?

MRS. PRIDDY. I can't see anything.

ANDY. Not near enough yet - this mist. Have to be by the houses there before you'd get a glimpse. What does it sound like?

MRS. PRIDDY. What?

ANDY. What they're coming in.

MRS. PRIDDY. I don't know.

BOY. There's only one of them.

ANDY. Eh?

BOY. - whatever it is.

(They listen)

OLD'UN. Mm.

TURK. A jeep, that's what it is, or a duck perhaps .

BOY. A what?

TURK. Like a tractor that can go on water, sort of. A duck.

ANDY. I int heard tell o' that before.

TURK. Ah well, life's full of little surprises, Andy Ipps.

BOY. Might be Mr. Churchill, come to give us a cigar. Heard
we was here and he's coming on his ol' chariot to get us.

TURK. Or cartloads of luscious women, voluptuous bints sent
for me little brother here. We old folk will just have to
close our eyes to what follows, won't we Mrs. P?

ANDY. Or it could be the Jerries.

(Sudden stop. They hadn't thought of that)

So let's not scream the place down till we know.

OLD'UN. Heh?

BOY. (quite shaken) It couldn't be, could it?

ANDY. Why not?

TURK. He's right. We don't know what's happened, do we?
They could have overrun the place by now. Right up to
London.

MRS. PRIDDY. Something there!

(They turn back to the windows)

 *(Outside. The noise of the duck is very loud. The vague
outlines of the vehicle can be seen drawing up in the middle
of the hamlet)

 *(Inside)

ANDY. Only one.

BOY. (who can't see) Only one what?

OLD'UN. Shush.

BOY. (whispering) Only one what?

DOD. Thing.

BOY. Eh?

*(Outside. The engine is switched off. Sudden silence, except for the lapping of the water which sounds clearer than ever before. /A man clambers out of the driver's seat into the water, which comes up to his knees)

*(Inside)

MRS. PRIDDY. He's got a gun.

ANDY. Yea?

OLD'UN. (screwing up his eyes shortsightedly) Anyone else there?

ANDY. Can't see no-one.

BOY. What's he look like?

TURK. Can't see.

BOY. Can't you see him?

ANDY. Just a...black shape.

BOY. What uniform? (no-one replies) Eh?

MRS. PRIDDY. (sharply) He's moving.

OLD'UN. Keep still.

BOY. (whisper) Is he a Jerry?

ANDY. (irritated) Can't see!

*(Outside. The man wades over to a house and looks in the door. The mist keeps the whole scene in silhouette, black shapes in the dimness)

*(Inside)

TURK. Well what're we going to do?

OLD'UN. Wait.

ANDY. Not call him ? Not...do anything?

OLD'UN. No.

MRS. PRIDDY. But he might go away!

    *(Outside. The man wades across to another house. His tommy gun can be seen under his arm)

    *(Inside)

TURK. A Jerry wouldn't have call to do that. If they was looking for snipers they'd have sent a squad. He's asking for trouble.

OLD'UN. Just leave it to -

TURK. Up you, mate, he's one of us, sent to get us!

ANDY. We couldn't load the boy onto that thing.

TURK. Eh?

ANDY. Look at it. Only hold three people at the most, sitting up. There's nowhere to lie the boy down. They wouldn't have sent that for us, with the injured boy.

TURK. Well who is he then?

    *(Outside. The man stands in the middle of the hamlet, looking about him. He suddenly calls out:)

MAN. Oooo...aaah...aaah!

    *(Inside)

BOY. What'd he say?

MRS. PRIDDY. What was it?

ANDY. Just a noise.

MRS. PRIDDY. What, German?

TURK. Don't think it was anything.

MRS. PRIDDY. If he was English, he'd have called out "Hallo".

TURK. Yes, but it wasn't German was it?

*(Outside)

MAN. (calls again) Ooo...aah...aah!

*(Inside)

MRS. PRIDDY. I'm going out to him.

OLD'UN. Stay still.

MRS. PRIDDY. I'm sorry Mr. Williams but we can't just -

TURK. Don't take anything from him, love, he don't know.

OLD'UN. Just hold it a minute can't you? - he might -

ANDY. Shush!

(In the distance, the deep note of a foghorn moans up, repeating at 30 second intervals)

DOD. Foghorn.

BOY. Eyah!

ANDY. What about that then.

BOY. They wouldn't do that if there was Germans about.

OLD'UN. Right.

MRS. PRIDDY. What happened to them all then?

TURK. It could be them, to guide their own shipping in, they started it.

(Pause. The foghorn sounds)

ANDY. Maybe we have give in.

BOY. Maybe they used poison gas. That's why we didn't hear nothing. Everyone dead, except us here.

(Pause. The foghorn sounds)

DOD. (at window) Coming here!

OLD'UN. Eh?

(ANDY looks out)

*(Outside. The man is wading towards the church)

*(Inside)

OLD'UN. Down, get down, all of you! Keep away from the
window. Behind the pew there -

TURK. The boy!

MRS. PRIDDY. Can't move him.

ANDY. I'll see to him.

OLD'UN. Quick!

(They hide in the boxpews. ANDY frantically covers THE BOY
with an old torn curtain and rubble)

OLD'UN. Get behind the pewend there. With any luck he'll just
look in and go. · Andy Ipps - behind the door, behind that there.

ANDY. Right.

OLD'UN. If I shout, get him.

MRS. PRIDDY. He's here!

DOD. Heee...eee!

(Silence. The man is heard, wading, approaching. He
crosses slowly past a window. The foghorn sounds. /DOD
and MRS. PRIDDY hold their breaths./ The man enters
stealthily, rifle at the ready. He is wearing a khaki
uniform but still cannot clearly be seen./ Suddenly TURK
speaks, in a perfectly normal voice)

TURK. (incredulous) He's black!

(THE MAN swings round, pointing his gun at the sound of the
voice. He is a Negro)

MAN. Uh?

TURK. He's a black man!

(TURK stands up)

Well, I'm...! Are you Hitler's secret weapon?

MAN. Don't move!

(The others slowly stand up)

MRS. PRIDDY. Well, I'll go to 'ell.

BOY. Jeez.

(They stare at him)

MAN. What you doing here?

TURK. Waiting for you, sweetheart. (moves forward; the man tenses) All right, all right, we won't eat you, we don't like missionary.

MAN. Go back there, that end. Go on. (to BOY) You too.

OLD'UN. He can't move. Didn't they tell you?

MAN. Eh?

OLD'UN. He's injured.

MAN. What's the matter with him?

OLD'UN. Broken ribs.

MAN. Oh?

(His uniform is smartly pressed, the buttons shining and trim)

Who's in charge here?

(OLD'UN. I am.   )
(   ) simultaneously
(TURK. Nobody is.   )

MAN. Not too sure, are you?

ANDY. (steps forward) Well, it's -

MAN. Don't move!

(Rigid pause)

MRS. PRIDDY. You are...one of us, aren't you?

MAN. Eh?

MRS. PRIDDY. You're ...British...Empire?

MAN. Course.

ANDY. Well then!

MRS. PRIDDY. Then you're one of us - you're on our side, aren't you?

MAN. (doesn't reply)

BOY. Where do you come from?

MAN. 203, Alfred Drive, Ashford, Kent.

BOY. You live there?

MAN. Course.

ANDY. Well then, I...don't see...why you... (he gestures to gun)

MAN. You British?

ANDY. Yes.

MAN. Six.

TURK. Yea.

MAN. Uhhuh.

    (He looks round)

    Why you wearing your night things?

OLD'UN. (forcibly) Look. We sent someone for help. This child's parents. To get help. We can't move him, see? Were you sent to -

    (THE BOY suddenly slumps forward on a pew)

(MAN. Don't move him - no, don't touch -   ) sim-
(   )

(MRS. PRIDDY. Keep his head up, mind he)
(don't strike it -)
( ) -ultaneously
(DOD. Boy, he alright?)

    (There is a spontaneous move by everybody. THE MAN has
    put his rifle down and is bending over the boy)

MAN. Keep off, now keep off. You moved him at all?

OLD'UN. No.

TURK. What do you know about it?

MAN. Cough up any blood?

OLD'UN. A little.

    (He feels THE BOY's chest gently. They watch him. The
    foghorn sounds)

ANDY. What do you know about it?

MAN. I trained.

TURK. In the Medics, are you?

MAN. No.

TURK. What then?

MAN. Local Defence Volunteers.

TURK. Amateurs!

MAN. I sergeant!

ANDY. What you doing here then?

MAN. (still working) It's my Assignment.

ANDY. What is?

    (Pause)

MAN. We can't move him.

OLD'UN. I know that.

MAN. (to OLD'UN) You ought to have got help.

OLD'UN. (reddening) Look -

ANDY. What's your Assignment?

MAN. Go through all the villages on the Marsh, see everyone has gone.

TURK. Because of the flooding.

MAN. Course.

MRS. PRIDDY. Who told you the invasion was on?

MAN. No-one told me.

OLD'UN. Then how do you know?

MAN. (pause: he looks up) Isn't it?

OLD'UN. Did you receive orders?

MAN. I heard the bombing. And someone rang the bells.

MRS. PRIDDY. Johnny Ipps.

MAN. Eh?

MRS. PRIDDY. Johnny Ipps, it was Johnny Ipps rang the bells.

TURK. Not the ones he must have heard.

OLD'UN. So you made your own way, didn't check with anyone first?

MAN. No.

MRS. PRIDDY. What about the other soldiers?

MAN. What about them?

MRS. PRIDDY. Well - you're a soldier, you must be in a barracks or -

MAN. I Local Defence, live at home.

ANDY. Well, collecting your... duck, then.

78

MAN. I keep that in the back garden.

(Pause)

TURK. At 203, Alfred Drive?

MAN. Yes.

TURK. On the back lawn, like?

MAN. In a little shed.

TURK. (delighted) Really?

(Silence. They look at each other. Hope of rescue finally dies. THE MAN straightens up)

ANDY. Did you find anyone else?

MAN. Where?

ANDY. In the other villages.

MAN. No, they all gone - straight away, I reckon.

MRS. PRIDDY. Nobody left.

MAN. No.

(ANDY IPPS and MRS. PRIDDY exchange glances)

ANDY. (licking lips) Then we'd better get moving, hadn't we?

TURK. What?

MAN. He can't be moved.

ANDY. Anyone can be moved.

MRS. PRIDDY. We're just like chicks here, aren't we? - like chicks.

ANDY. We're not going to get another chance.

(Pause)

OLD'UN. (dully) We're staying here.

DOD. You're not well, Mr. Williams. (OLD'UN looks up; DOD speaks gently) You're not well.

(Pause. THE OLD'UN turns quietly away. Silence)

MAN. (to ANDY) Can you drive?

ANDY. Yea.

MAN. Drive to Appledore Camp, get an M.O. and an amphibious ambulance.

ANDY. What, in your -

MAN. It drives like a tractor. You drive a tractor?

ANDY. Yes.

MAN. Right.

(Pause)

DOD. Back before you know we're gone.

ANDY. No-one else?

(They look at OLD'UN: he is apart from them all, in the chancel, his back to them. Slowly and quietly he is lifting masonry and attempting to replace it how it was before./The foghorn breathes its deep note. The stone chinks as he moves it./They go quietly)

MAN. Some of them things.

TURK. Eh?

MAN. (gestures to hassocks)

TURK. Oh.

(They prop THE BOY into a slightly more comfortable position on the floor where he fell./ The duck starts up outside: they listen)

*(Outside. ANDY IPPS, DOD and MRS. PRIDDY, clinging onto the duck, their faces set. The vehicle grinds forward through the water. They disappear into the mist)

80

*(Inside. OLD'UN lifts a stone back into place and holds it there. Silence)

TURK. (suddenly) How about a fire, what about a little fire, eh? - warm us all up. (he busies himself; OLD'UN turns and looks at THE BOY) See if we can squeeze a little heat out of this old place, should burn, this stuff, it's old enough.

OLD'UN. Lips are blue.

MAN. Breathing funny.

OLD'UN. Cold?

TURK. (fast) Nice bowl of hot soup, and a warm bottle of rum, that's what we want. Be like Christmas. Be rather nice to spend Christmas here, wouldn't it Sambo, know about Christmas do you? How do you celebrate it at 203 Alfred Drive? Eat the neighbours?

OLD'UN. You a medical man?

MAN. I know about these things.

TURK. (piling the firewood) Tough lot in Ashford, I'd say. I know one or two bints that'd probably be pretty good rissoles, though. How do you reckon, professionally speaking, that Mr. Williams here would make out as a goulash?

OLD'UN. (eyeing him curiously) Where do you come from?

MAN. Ashford. (looks at him) I told you that.

(THE BOY stirs)

OLD'UN. Moving.

MAN. Ah.

OLD'UN. Look at him!

(THE BOY moves again. OLD'UN is looking at him as if he had never seen him before. He watches his limbs moving and stirring delicately./TURK watches too: and

finally accepts that THE BOY will not recover. /He puts a
light to the fire. As the flames creep up, THE BOY opens his
eyes)

BOY. Oh, a fire!

TURK. There she blows!

BOY. What's going on?

TURK. Yes well, I thought we might all have a nice cosy evening
together, with cold wet drizzle coming through the roof, and
The Old'Un here to tell us tales of funerals long ago.

OLD'UN. You warm, bird?

BOY. Yes, ta. Look - you can't tell dusk when there's a fog can
you? - the light just...drains away. What happened?

MAN. Had a faint, nothing to worry about.

BOY. Where are the others?

OLD'UN. They're gone.

BOY. Gone?

OLD'UN. To get help.

BOY. (simple acceptance) Oh. You a doctor?

MAN. Local Defence Volunteer.

BOY. Ah.

MAN. I the first to join.

BOY. Were you?

OLD'UN. Why?

MAN. Eh?

OLD'UN. Why were you the first to join?

MAN. (eyes narrowing) Why shouldn't I be?

TURK. Why did you join at all?

MAN. To...Defend Our Shores Against the Invader.

(Pause)

TURK. Yea?

MAN. (furious outburst) What so wrong with that, heh? - I
fight for King and Country, see, and British Heritage,
hooray, I am true Briton, God Save the King!

(TURK and THE OLD'UN are fascinated)

BOY. Hey - watch it, you're treading on a bit of British
Heritage.

MAN. Heh?

(He steps back, revealing the brass)

BOY. They're Ippses, very old.

MAN. What is that?

BOY. Ippses, related to Mr. Ipps you met, they lived here.

MAN. (prickly) What you mean, they live here?

BOY. Here, in Old Romney, they lived here.

MAN. Oh? (peers at them) I aint seen no-one like that around
here.

BOY. No - a long time ago, this was.

MAN. (suspicious) Which house they live in?

BOY. I dunno.

MAN. You don't know much, do you?

(The four of them are crouched round the fire, now on equal
terms, warming their hands. The foghorn moans outside)

TURK. You married, Sambo?

MAN. (tetchy) Why shouldn't I be married?

TURK. Well, are you?

MAN. Sure, of course I married, naturally.

BOY. What, a...like you?

MAN. She British, sure, like me.

BOY. (after working that one out) Yes, but a... (horrid search)...negress?

MAN. No, she third cousin to an honourable.

TURK. An honourable what?

MAN. An honourable, you know, younger child of a peer.

TURK. You're kidding.

MAN. That was Lord Coope, see; his grandfather's brother was the 16th Marquis of Devon, the King's second cousin.

(Stunned pause)

BOY. What does that make you?

MAN. Don't make me anything.

BOY. Int you got no castle?

TURK. They got 203 Alfred Drive.

MAN. That's it!

TURK. (who has been studying the brass) Hey - well what do you know! Do you know who this says is down here? Johnny Ipps.

BOY. Garn.

TURK. S'true - look - "Pray for the soules of John Ipps" - see? Who's the bird then? Looks a bit of an old wreck to me. Still, old Johnny Ipps can't afford to pick and choose, can he? Well, what do you know! - that's where he's been all the time! (bangs on the tomb) Aye Johnny Ipps, that's enough, leave her alone you filthy beast, come up, we're onto you!

BOY. There's a string of letters at the end here. M and a D,

I think that is, and Cs. (he tries to pronounce it)
"Mmdclxxviii" What do you reckon that means?

TURK. It's a very rude word, in Latin. What the Pope said
when he caught the Cardinal having it off with a vatican.
Crafty lot, these old Micks - they don't wear anything
under all them frocks, you know, just like Scotsmen.

BOY. You ever been married, Mr. Williams?

OLD'UN. (after a pause) No.

BOY. (chattering on) I'm going to marry when I'm twenty-one.
Least, I'm going to announce my engagement on my twenty-
first birthday party.

TURK. All worked out, eh?

BOY. More or less. I'll have saved £84.12s. by then on my
present rate of pay. Do you think that's enough?

TURK. Who's the girl?

BOY. Oh, I haven't tied myself down to anyone yet. I've got
someone in mind, but I'm not sure if she's really right. I
mean, you've got to be realistic about these things, haven't
you?

TURK. Isn't no-one going to ask me if I'm going to get married?

MAN. Are you?

TURK. No sir, I'm happy as I am. Me, I'm never going to
marry.

OLD'UN. Huh!

BOY. Well, what are you going to do about... well, "you-know-
what"?

TURK. About what?

BOY. "You-know-what".

TURK. What's he talking about?

MAN. Sex, I think.

TURK. Are you?

BOY. Well...I suppose... yes.

TURK. What do you mean, you suppose?

BOY. (terribly awkward) Yes, I do mean......sex.

TURK. That's better. Don't you worry about me and my "you-know-what", matey, I can look after myself. (putting more wood on the fire)

BOY. (with attempted delicacy) What sort of young lady are you looking for to walk out with?

TURK. Aye aye, he's coming out of his shell fast, isn't he? Can't hold this impetuous young generation any more, the air's blue wherever they're around. Why most of them are drinking beer before they're thirty. Shall I tell you what sort of young lady I am looking for to walk out with?

BOY. Yes, go on.

TURK. OK; I know, cos I saw her once. Walking down Bethnal Green Road I was. Lots of little old houses down there. Anyhow, I looked in one window, and there was a kitchen, - see, in the front facing onto the street; and there was a beautiful black mammy, plenty of her, you know, frying two eggs in a pan.

(Pause)

BOY. Well, go on.

TURK. That's all.

MAN. Frying two eggs in a pan.

TURK. That's right.

(Pause. Abruptly, OLD'UN starts to splutter and cough. His frame shakes and rolls, his face creased up, and he rolls his body with delight. He is laughing./ THE BOY and TURK look at him with amazed amusement./ THE OLD'UN booms and shakes. THE NEGRO joins in. They rock back and forth)

BOY. You know, Mr. Williams, that's the first time I ever seen you laugh!

(THE OLD'UN, rocking and roaring, ruffles his hair: then

splutters off again, quaking with mirth./ The foghorn sounds.
They are in a warm pool of light, in the rapidly falling
darkness. Fade)

(There is a long, deep boom that seems to fill the sky and
hang in the air./ The votive lamp, still alight but hanging
lopsided and cracked, shivers with the impact./ The sound
repeats, like the slow full-muffled note of a huge bell./ They
run to a window and look out)

*(Outside. Visibility is down to a few yards. The water is
agitated and ripples with small waves)

*(Inside)

BOY. Look - look -

(He indicates the everyday door of the church, through which
water gushes. OLD'UN, SAMBO and TURK run to block it)

(OLD'UN. Some of them there, the hassocks, them books)
(- move! Books nigger! You (to TURK) help here.)
(   ) sim.
(TURK. Above waterlevel, eh? Built right above the -)
(You sad old man. Why pretend? - what's the point?)

(They overturn the font, jam the broken side of a pew against
the door and heave the font against it./ SAMBO runs back and
forth with armfuls of blockage, vestments, altar clothes,
crosses, huge old bibles, hymnbooks, all the paraphernalia
of established Christianity. Together they block the door
from the slowly rising water)

BOY. There too look - in the tower, in the wall look -

(Water gushes through a hole there also. SAMBO runs and
stuffs it with old cassocks. /The three men turn inwards,
panting, searching the walls and floor for further inlets./
The sound repeats, a deep muffled noise, filling the sky)

TURK. Any more for the Skylark!

(Plaster falls in the chancel and water sprays in: TURK shouts
and runs to stop it. /OLD'UN sits heavily by THE BOY)

BOY. What's that noise, Mr. Williams?

OLD'UN. (stares ahead, panting)

BOY. Like a bell, sort of bell. What's it mean?

(TURK and SAMBO together lift a huge beam and stack it against the inlet)

OLD'UN. We'll be over the water here. Little hillocks they built -

(TURK and SAMBO run into the tower area and heave away old woodwork to stack against inlets. The deep noise sounds again, muffled, bell-like)

- when they curbed and walled off the sea. Was the bed of the sea here, see, the whole Marsh, men had to block it off to live here at all, built dykes and seawalls to keep it back, stem it.

(TURK and SAMBO ram the woodwork against the north door. A loose beam falls, plaster cracks away in lumps from the walls)

Still belongs, though! - you can feel it trying to get back. Fog, like now, lowlying close to the ground, sort of ghost of the sea that belongs here: you watch the sea a rough day, against the dykes - pounding at it, shouting "I'm coming back, I'm coming, you'll see!"

(The note sounds again. TURK and SAMBO batter stone into place, block and jam. There is now a half-inch of water all over the floor. More sections of the mural are seen, more faces)

But that doesn't stop people - fighting it, pounding it back with every ounce and every breath. It's God's Logick it stays out - we must know we'll win, we're too strong for it, hammer it, we'll stem it, God's logick!

(Part of the chancel roof grinds in, a beam and a shower of rubble)

"Or who shut up the sea with doors, when it brake forth, as if it had issued out of the womb?

(TURK and SAMBO pound and stow, ramming the stone into place. The sound repeats, a huge deep note, filling the sky)

"When I brake up for it my decreed place, and set bars
and doors, And said, Hitherto shalt thou come, but no
further: and here shall thy proud waves be stayed?!"

(There is a roar, as if a wave actually broke against the
church: the building vibrates, and the water can be heard
rushing round outside the walls that protect them)

BOY. Look!

(On one side of the tower arch, more plaster has fallen away,
revealing part of a gigantic face: although several feet
across, only the immense eye is revealed, huge, noble and
lifeless. Its size is such that the entire face, if revealed,
could not begin to fit into the tiny church.

The sea roars again and is heard to break against the
building. Plaster falls, the blockage erected by TURK and
SAMBO shivers.

There comes a gentle and regular knocking at the west door,
as if something floating on the water was being washed to and
fro against it, striking it)

OLD'UN. (shouts) There! There!

TURK. Eh?

OLD'UN. They're come, they're here! Let them in -

(He runs to the west door and starts to grapple with the bolts
and bars)

TURK. Bloody madman, what's he doing - (shouts) There's
nobody there!

(OLD'UN. There is, there is, can't you hear them? -)
(Help me!   )
(   ) sim.
(TURK. But we would have heard them coming,   )
(wouldn't we?   )

OLD'UN. Here nigger - Move!

(SAMBO helps him)

BOY. Turk?

TURK. Hallo.

BOY. It's not no-one, is it?

TURK. No.

BOY. Is he a bit...?

TURK. He's sick.

(At the door they struggle: OLD'UN crashes a stone down on a strut: it splits apart)

TURK. What's that you've got?

BOY. Eh?

TURK. In your hand.

(THE BOY holds out a piece of stone the size of a walnut)

BOY. Fossil.

TURK. (admiring) Ah!

BOY. Good, innit? Look, it's a fern leaf.

TURK. Yea.

BOY. That's hundreds of millions of years old, that is. It's just curling open, look. This was growing on the surface of the earth once, then it got buried under the sea. Plants and things do that, if they're very old. And animals.

TURK. And fish. There was a little fish like that at school.

BOY. Same school as I...

TURK. (nodding) Snargit school. Outside Miss Otley's room.

BOY. (pause) I hardly know you, do I? (pause) Why did you come back Turk?

TURK. I dunno. Bloody mad. First place they'll look for me here, the Redcaps. I just come, that's all, when all this - (he gestures) - started. I just had to come.

(Pause)

BOY. Look, isn't it smashing, just uncurling. Bet once it was crushed it reckoned it hadn't got a future.

TURK. A future?

BOY. Ayeh. Here - you take it.

TURK. Bit of rock?

BOY. Fernleaf. Put it in your pocket.

> (TURK pockets it. His brother smiles at him, sadly./ The west door bursts open and there is a rush of water inwards. The two men are forced back to the sides of the tower. /On the crest of the flush of water, riding it as if he had forced the door open, is the body of a drowned man./ TURK rises and stares)

OLD'UN. (rapidly) Here, nigger, take his shoulder, come on! (to body) All right lad, all right, we've got you, we're here -

SAMBO. But he's - but he's -

OLD'UN. Move man, get hold of his shirt, shirt, quick! -

SAMBO. (does so, sobbing)

OLD'UN. Heeeeee...

> (They pull him clear of the water, over the step, onto the floor of the nave)

BOY. (as they do this) Who - who is it?

TURK. (stands silent)

OLD'UN. Turn him over, quick, quick - move that, space to turn him - You're here now Johnny, we've got you son, soon have you good as new - gently, now, steady -

BOY. Johnny Ipps? Is it? (TURK stands silent) Turk!

TURK. (quietly) Yes.

> (They turn him over. Half his chest has been blown away leaving an appalling hole where his heart and lungs once were)

SAMBO. (standing) Ah...

TURK. (closes his eyes)

(Silence)

BOY. (quietly) Is that... it?

OLD'UN. (suddenly bursting into activity again) You - pile of
hassock stuff for under his stomach, lift his middle, see,
drain the water out. (to TURK) Six inch strips, that curtain,
rip it. And some white cloth.

(They stare at him. He is feverishly stripping off his coat)

(sobbing) You knew we was here all along, didn't you bird?
You were warning us, weren't you, trying to tell us?

(He stuffs his coat under JOHNNY's head, and tears chunks
of his own shirt away to wipe his face)

I knew you wouldn't let us down, not you, oh-ho no! There -
there - so - so. Oh my baby, we'll have you singing yet!

TURK. (quietly) Mr. Williams.

OLD'UN. (shouts) Come on, jump - where are you, he's hurt!

TURK. Listen -

OLD'UN. (furious) Blust, do I talk to myself? Help, can't you
help him!

SAMBO. Mister, he's not -

OLD'UN. (turning on him) Any soft stuff in that pile, eh? - must
be. And fresh water, clean.

TURK. (shouts) Look at him! - just look at him, look!

OLD'UN. (turning violently on TURK) You don't care, do you,
it doesn't mean anything to you -

(OLD'UN talks right through TURK in a desperate attempt
not to hear him:-)

(TURK. Why don't you just open your eyes? Just look,   )
(look at him that's all! No, you just don't want to know,)   sim-
(do you -   )

92

(OLD'UN. - but it's all there is! We can make him well) ⌐
(again, it can be alright, but I need help, you must) | -ultaneously
(help -)

(In full flood, TURK suddenly takes THE OLD'UN's wrist in
both his hands and plunges it into the huge wound in JOHNNY
IPPS' chest./ OLD'UN screams and writhes to be released./
SAMBO screeches in his own language./ TURK holds
OLD'UN like a vice, his eyes boring into his face)

TURK. (through clenched teeth) Look! look! look! look!
look!

(SAMBO throws himself down on his face, shivering, his
own language pouring out of him.

OLD'UN sees, and goes limp, staring at JOHNNY. TURK
releases him./SAMBO stops./ Long pause./ Gently, OLD'UN
takes his hand from the wound, and lifts himself up to his
full height. Silence./He looks at TURK)

OLD'UN. (very quietly) I'm not going to cry, you know. It's
been too.... Magnificent!

(He turns away. TURK covers JOHNNY with a torn curtain:
it is too short, so he covers the wound, leaving the thin
white face exposed./OLD'UN sits slowly, near the open west
door, his hand on his injured arm. He stares ahead of
him.
The foghorn starts up again, a quiet breathing, quieter than
the bell-noise by far. / TURK picks up a stone and throws it
violently against the wall. / SAMBO lies face downwards,
shivering violently and silently. THE BOY makes a naive
effort to comfort him)

BOY. Hey - Sambo - Sambo. It's all right, we're going to be
alright you know! There's no invasion, or they wouldn't
have started up that old foghorn again, would they? Hey,
listen to it. And the water. Like we was all on a ship out
in the fog, isn't it? - bound for the Sunny Isles. Can't you
feel us moving? - the wind heaving along them sails aloft?
(calls out) Where we bound, Mr. Williams? - and when do
we arrive?

(Pause. TURK lobs a stone or two, halfheartedly, then
stops./THE OLD'UN stares before him, his lips moving
silently./The countless faces of the mural, and the one huge
one, stare down)

BOY. Eh Sambo.

SAMBO. Mm?

BOY. Will you help me, tell me something?

SAMBO. What's that?

BOY. Well - it's something I wanted to ask you about, see. And I don't know how to... I mean, you may think I've been around a lot, but I haven't, not really. I'm not... well, I'm not...

SAMBO. Eh?

BOY. You know - I haven't... "you-know-what".

SAMBO. (after a pause) Oh.

BOY. Well...

SAMBO. Yes?

BOY. Are you... all right with her?

SAMBO. Eh?

BOY. - your wife. Are you alright with your wife?

SAMBO. How all right?

BOY. Well.... "you-know-what".

SAMBO. Oh.

BOY. Well?

SAMBO. She good to me.

BOY. Yea?

> (Pause. TURK quietly sings the line of the song: it is sad, resigned. He sits huddled in his old choirstall, staring at the fossil in his hand)

SAMBO. But it not good here - in this country, this place.

BOY. No?

SAMBO. The room too cold, see.

BOY. Oh. That's important, is it?

SAMBO. Yes.

BOY. Oh (he makes a mental note)

SAMBO. After the war, 1919, the Government told me to come here. That the Government of Gold Coast, see. Everything on paper then, you know, documents and things. So I come. And here I marry. But we not happy here.

BOY. Why didn't you go back then?

SAMBO. (after a pause) I don't know.

BOY. But you get on alright... privately, don't you?

SAMBO. (wriggling) Yes.

BOY. (gently probing) Yes?

SAMBO. She all right.

BOY. Aren't you sure?

SAMBO. Sure I sure, sure I sure.

BOY. You do... "you-know-what"?

SAMBO. Boyey, you please...

BOY. (immediately) Oh sorry, I didn't...

(They are both acutely embarrassed by this conversation: but stronger than that is the desire to talk about intimate things at this time./ TURK sings again, quiet, sad, a dying fall./ THE OLD'UN stares into space, muttering almost inaudibly)

OLD'UN. (muttering) ...walking five miles for a ha'penny worth of spices, no roads then, just green fields, green...

SAMBO. (after a struggle) We... "you-know-what" - Yes. OK?

BOY. Oh. It's alright, isn't it? Not... difficult, or anything?

SAMBO. Sure it alright.

BOY. Is it hard to... learn?

SAMBO. No no. Easy. (he shuffles uncomfortably) Easy.

BOY. What's up then?

SAMBO. Nothing up.

BOY. You seem funny about it.

SAMBO. Who funny?

BOY. Don't you like talking about it?

SAMBO. I got nothing 'gainst it.

> (Pause. TURK sings quietly. SAMBO and THE BOY are leaning against a long Latin inscription on a monument: the harsh, black classical lettering runs behind their heads, death)

BOY. It's alright then, is it?

SAMBO. Yes.

BOY. I dream about it, you know. I'm going to have lots of it when we get away from here. That's Life, isn't it? That's being... well, that's being a Man!

> (SAMBO looks at him: for the first time, we see him thinking something he doesn't say. He looks away.
> TURK stands up quietly, watching them and moving as unobtrusively as possible, but with new resolution. He has stopped singing. He looks long at his brother: then at OLD'UN. / Cut to his point of view: OLD'UN's chest: a mass of thick blood is seeping through his torn shirt. Tilt up to his face: his head is back against the wall, and he stares at the fractured roof, absolutely motionless. With eyes wide open, the tears are slowly and silently moving down his face)

SAMBO. Boyo.

BOY. Yea?

SAMBO. I talk to you - man to man, see.

BOY. Yea?

SAMBO. Well... (a struggle)... I don't know.

96

BOY. Eh?

SAMBO. I don't know if it good.

BOY. Don't know?

SAMBO. I don't know cos I aint... "you-know-what"...with anyone else. I think she alright, but I don't know see.

BOY. Oh.

SAMBO. I tell you; I marry her for - "you-know-what". I don't like talk, see. And man, I don't like her no more. You ask what up, well, that's what's up. She wasn't very beautiful when I married her and well - she aint improved any. I not very clever, and I not very beautiful myself, so I reckon I was lucky. She worked in a caff, I used to have tea there; so one day when I give her threepence for my tea I said "Will you marry me" and she said "All right" and them's the first words we spoke. That fourteen years ago.

(Pause)

(suddenly) But we us, see?

BOY. Don't you... I mean, isn't there anyway you can...It sounds a bit, well... dull.

SAMBO. (dully) It all right.

BOY. She doesn't... you couldn't... well, sort of brighten it up a bit?

SAMBO. Well, I don't know. I tried once, but it didn't do no good. It too cold here, see. We just sort of accept, now. Somehow we just give up. Give it up. Trying, you know.

(THE BOY stirs, delicately, uneasily.

TURK quietly moves out through the open west door, barely visible in the thickening fog which rapidly swallows him up. He makes no sound./We see JOHNNY IPPS' dead face: and the crowded murals watching)

OLD'UN. (muttering to himself) When I was a chick... the world was full of apples...

(There is a distant sound like a long, deep boom carried on

the wind from far off, muffled by the mist. The foghorn
sounds, deep and long.

We see the three men waiting, resigned, motionless. They
look almost like men lying awake at night, staring at the
ceiling.

The water laps, creeping up with infinite slowness. The
waves are becoming longer sweeps, part of the open sea.
Fade)

The Rhyme   (See page 57)

Mrs. Butler, dealer in stamps,
Over the road they take in tramps.
Jimmy Jordan, good shoemaker,
Thomas Bayley, an excellent baker.

At the corner, full of people,
Mrs. Terry's jam and treacle
Dr. Proctor's, cut and bruises
Pink pills for very general uses.

In the lane there's shrimps and fishes
Mrs. Jell's for plates and dishes
Mrs. Collins for a cake, and
Mr. Judd to undertake.

BATTLE AT TEMATANGI

BATTLE AT TEMATANGI was first presented on BBC-1
Television on February 3rd, 1971, with the following cast:

TURK	Mike Pratt
ANNA	Anne Stallybrass
WILLY	Anthony May
BECK	Ian Hogg
DOOLAN	George Sewell
THORPE	James Cosmo
RATS	Geoffrey Hughes
AJUS I	Ronald Eng
GRAMPS	Mei Yuan Chong
AJUS II	Jimmy Fung
CAPTAIN	Leo Britt
THE GIRL	Keri Emmerson
THE OLD MAN	Chong Choy

The play was produced by Mark Shivas

The play was directed by Robert Knights

(The East Caroline Islands, off the Philippines, 28th of
February, 1954.

A confused and sporadic civil war is in progress in a series
of guerilla encounters. The anti-government forces are
amateur and ragged: they contain squads of foreign volunteers
and mercenaries, particularly Europeans. Most of the local
population is trying to stay neutral and uninvolved.

A scattered guerilla force, with some local civilians, retrea-
ting up a scrub-covered hillside towards a small farm, firing
scrappily as they go to cover their retreat. / Uniformed
troops in the village below fire after them. Dozens of
civilians, particularly children, lie wounded or run
shrieking for shelter. There has been an ambush and a
school is in the main line of fire between the two sides. / The
farm: some of the unit snipe down at the village to cover the
rest, who run for an old lorry on the far side of the farmyard.
They load ammunition and equipment and climb aboard,
helping the injured. The lorry backs with a roar. / The
remainder jump on except for one - TURK - who continues
to empty his tommygun with a sort of frenzy, on the troops
below. The lorry moves off. / TURK stands right up,
whirls his gun by its barrel around his head and hurls it with
all his strength down at the village with a yell. He runs and
jumps onto the lorry at speed as it leaves the farmyard.
There is a roar and a shell explodes where they had been.

*Inside the lorry. Lurching along at high speed. They have
to shout to be heard)

WILLY. (driving) Heading for Xewkija, alright?

(BECK. Just get out, get out of this lot -   )
(   )
(DOOLAN. Yes, along the coast, contact MHQ -   )   sim.
(   )
(THORPE. I don't know that we, er, ought to make -)

ANNA. (explosion) But we can't just run out on the whole job!

BECK. Then what do you reckon, brighteyes?

ANNA. Join up with the other squads, go in when they do -

```
(BECK.  Don't be bloody stupid.              )
(                                            )
(RAPS.  I don't think we should do that -    )  sim.
(                                            )
(DOOLAN.  What, back into that?              )
```

THORPE. Seven other groups like us scattered just anywhere in eight hundred square miles of jungle -

BECK. Yea!

THORPE. - how do we find them? How do we know they didn't run into what we did?

DOOLAN. Back to the coast round Xewkija, contact Mobile HQ when they land tomorrow, that's the ticket -

THORPE. (uncertain) Well...

ANNA. What for, what's the point?

DOOLAN. Orders, woman, the what-now, from GHQ! -

BECK. - black bastards, a lot they'll say -

DOOLAN. - no officers among us, are there? - nothing we can do. Only a twenty mile stretch of coast, with any luck we'll find MHQ party when they land in the morning.

BECK. Needle in a bloody haystack, it's thick jungle that whole stretch of coast.

RAPS. We'll be safe there then.

BECK. Eh?

RAPS. We'll be safe there.

ANNA. So we just rat out on the whole operation, just -

```
(BECK.  Yes, just that thing.                )
(                                            )
(DOOLAN.  Use your bloody head woman -       )  sim.
```

(THORPE. I don't see what else -   )

TURK. (outburst) Look, we're lucky to have got out of that lot
at all, alright? No opposition they said, just a few wogs with
bows and arrows playing at soldiers - just walk straight in,
join up with the local boys and hey presto the place'll be
ours in an hour. And what happens? - the whole Imperial
bloody Army waiting for us bayonets fixed, and every bloody
bong in the local so-called underground army running like
rabbits at the first tiny pop -

(ANNA. Don't be so silly as to think -   )
(   ) sim.
(TWO LOCALS. (torrent of Malay)   )

TURK. (shouting almost hysterically) Shut up, shut
up, tell them to shut up!

(AJUS II calls out with pain: ANNA goes to him)

DOOLAN. You didn't exactly help, did you?

TURK. I'll say I didn't, boy.

BECK . And who did you think you were throwing your bloody
firearm at, eh? - think you're in a bloody film?

TURK. And here, you can have these too - (he throws over his
ammo pouches) - I'm not sweating my guts out for worse-
than-bloody-animals that just... those poor bastard kids!

WILLY. Aye.

TURK. You'd think they'd tell them, wouldn't you? - warn
them there was going to be a shoot-up in their schoolyard,
so they could clear out and -

DOOLAN. It was an ambush, son, the Imperial Army ambushed
us; they had to let things go on normal, we'd have noticed
else.

TURK. I know, I know, but - kids, eh? Always the kids, intit,
always the poor bastard kids.

THORPE. All this should have been planned for.

RAPS. What?

THORPE. - if things went wrong, there should have been a plan.

BECK. (derisive)

(THORPE. No? Wouldn't they -)
( ) sim.
(RAPS. Shouldn't there -)

BECK. Of course there should, but this pile of niggers wouldn't
    think of that, would they?

RAPS. Captain Onwalu'd know wouldn't he? - if there was one.

(THORPE. Yes, you'd think so -)
( )
(BECK. Don't talk to me about him -) sim.
( )
(DOOLAN. Huh! Him.)

TURK. And Captain burning Onwalu disappeared so fast come the
    fighting, you couldn't see the whites of his big fat feet for
    dust!

BECK. - bastard, the great c -

THORPE. But we don't know he was running away, he might
    have been -

(TURK. He what? - what do you -)
( )
(DOOLAN. What's he say?) sim.
( )
(BECK. Don't give me that! -)

TURK. He's one of them, int he? - in it for what he can get out
    of it, the biggest wog this side of the black stump bar none.
    In the real Army, officers used to count for something -
    (DOOLAN and BECK agree) - but with a pack of Boy-Scout-
    bloody-amateurs like this lot you're right out on your own;
    they didn't appoint no NCOs among us, didn't trust us
    like, or too bloody ignorant; so now our little nigger
    minstrel officer's done a bunk, that's it, we're on our tiny
    tods. You can go back into that lot if you want, but there's
    no-one tells me what I do, not any more; so -

(THORPE. (quickly) Look, we'd better have some sort) over-
(of...)
( ) -

(TURK. - so right, darlings, I'm getting <u>out</u>!   )
(   )
(THORPE. ...system, agreement, now we're on our   )
(own; for mutual, er -   )
(   )
(TURK. Oh don't give me all that guff -   )
(   )
(DOOLAN. Look, shut it, just shut it will you? - give)
(him a -   )
(   )
(TURK. - I don't owe anyone anything!   )

-lapping

THORPE. If we're going to - get through we can't just,
    er, all do what we...you know...

DOOLAN. Yea.

THORPE. We've got to - we're in this <u>together</u>, we've got to
    realise that. To <u>survive</u>. Don't <u>you think</u>? I mean, if what
    we're fighting for <u>means</u> anything, now's the time to practice
    it! Equality, fraternity, all that... What we're all here for.

    (Slight pause)

    I appeal to your good sense -

BECK. Anyhow we can't make Xewkija in this wagon.

DOOLAN. Why not?

BECK. Sixty miles? How do we get sixty miles in this, ey?
    (he bangs it with his hand) - <u>and</u> they'll be scouring every
    bush for us from here to Hongkong by now.

RAPS. We came on foot, too, through the bush -

THORPE. So?

RAPS. - I mean, do we even know the way? - by track like?
    <u>And</u> we had someone to guide us before.

WILLY. I've got a bump - (taps forehead) - of direction.

BECK. Well it better be a good one.

THORPE. What do <u>you</u> two reckon we should do then?

(BECK. (hastily) Don't ask me, I'm not a...)
(   ) sim.

105

(RAPS. Oh well, I'm not one to, erm -   )   sim.

TURK. Ha!

WILLY. But you're in it too.

BECK. Eh?

WILLY. (looking at DOOLAN) - what do you say?

DOOLAN. (wriggling) Yes, well it's difficult isn't it.

WILLY. We're all in this. All of us. No officer to hold your hand
   now.

   (At the far end of the truck TURK finds several more
   islanders huddled together, frightened: they include a young
   girl and a very old man, both injured and unconscious)

TURK. (explosion) And who the hell's this?

ANNA. (flat) Here when we came.

TURK. You what? All of them?

AJUS. Here in the truck like now.

TURK. Oh that's all we want intit? - a few more passengers.
   Look at them, they don't care a nigger's fart, do they?
   (he shouts into the face of one of them) I risked my bloody
   life to back your Glorious Revolution to the hilt, risked
   being shot to pieces for you! I must have been... and you
   just run! Look at you - stupid, stupid! (frantic) How do you
   think, ey? - what goes on in those fuzzy little minds?

BECK. Bang the buggers over the head and chuck them out.
   (silence) Listen, they'd have been quite happy to see us
   carved up.

THORPE. I don't think we should just -

DOOLAN. You say then.

THORPE. Eh?

DOOLAN. You say what to do with them.

THORPE. No need to - do anything to them, just - drop them
   off somewhere.

BECK. Oh very clever, run back and tell the Imperial Army all
106

about us, eh, and where we're going?

RAPS. (looking at THORPE) Yea.

(Pause)

WILLY. They couldn't help it.

TURK. Come again?

WILLY. They're like kids themselves.

THORPE. Eight of them.

DOOLAN. I saw three cop it. That tall fella, and that Chinese-looking couple. One got a mortar right through the belly.

BECK. Wham!

TURK. Yea, and all the rest run.

ANNA. (shouts) Alright, we heard you!

TURK. What's the matter with you?

ANNA. He's hurt, this man's hurt, give it a rest can't you?!

(She is bandaging AJUS II who is seriously wounded)

BECK. Int we got any food? Eh? Any food, have we?

(Pause)

TURK. What do they think we do it for!

DOOLAN. For £200 a month tax free.

TURK. Ha!

BECK. You'll never see that.

RAPS. What? We'll get paid, we've got to, it's in our contracts!

BECK. Should have asked for it before you put out.

RAPS. Did you?

BECK. Course.

RAPS. And they give it you?

BECK. They give me half.

RAPS. Here, it's in writing, look (he produces contract from inner pocket) I've got it here -

TURK. (suddenly) Why should I worry. I just want out. Out, no more! (indicating the wogs) Like that lot. Enough. Finish.

RAPS. (muttering through)"... and every fourth week the aforementioned... er..." - here somewhere...

(Pause)

TURK. (to AJUS) Hey you. You! What did he run for?

AJUS. Eh?

TURK. Captain burning Onwalu. Why did he run?

AJUS. Frightened.

DOOLAN. You have to laugh though. All his medals clanking like cowbells. He turned green that first shot.

BECK. It's all fun to them, isn't it, until it starts to rain.

(They lurch along, engine screaming. The OLD WOMAN rests the LITTLE GIRL's head on some sacking. The OLD MAN lies motionless. Suddenly everyone is near dead with sleep)

*(The lorry roars past on a jungle track: it is nearly dusk.)

*(Inside again. TURK pulling off the crude regimental flashes from the rough uniform they all wear. The rest lie out, asleep. The lorry bounds and crashes along. The OLD WOMAN, who could be the GIRL's grandmother, a mountain of a woman with a face like a bulldog, sits over the old man and the girl, tending them)

GRAN. (stream of Malay to TURK)

TURK. I don't speak it darling.

GRAN. (Malay, indicating OLD MAN)

108

TURK. Yes, love, one of your mob. Big man, big. He's
alright, not injured is he, just a bit shook up I expect. He
don't know what it's all about, does he? - nothing much ever
kept him lying awake nights (he jerks off his identity disc)
Fancy him, do you?

GRAN. (Malay, indicating TURK's gun and the YOUNG GIRL)

TURK. Yes, well it's me, innit, what I do. I mean, used to.
In the blood or something. Been doing it a long time now.

GRAN. (Malay)

TURK. (silence)

GRAN. (Malay)

TURK. I've run out before now. (pause) Haven't even scratched
the surface. (pause) Finish, out.

(He throws flashes and disc out of the lorry. We see him
close, now: he is 36, deeply baffled and tired to death. His
energy is now something he has to whip up, rather than
finding himself riding spontaneously on a great full surf-
wave of it. He looks down at the unconscious OLD MAN on
the floor)

TURK. Yes, he's alright.

*(Lorry roars past on the track. It is moonlight and we can
see glimpses of the sea close by, some way below, through
the trees. The lorry suddenly lurches, and stops abruptly)

*WILLY. Something there, down on the water.

RAPS. (waking) Eh? We there?

WILLY. In the water, by the shore.

THORPE. Boat?

WILLY. Could have been.

(They each momentarily wait for someone else to take the
initiative)

DOOLAN. Better - er - better have a shufti.

(TURK, THORPE, DOOLAN, BECK and WILLY pick up their arms and climb painfully out of the truck)

RAPS. I'll hold the fort.

WILLY. Keep them quiet, then, this lot.

(Several islanders in the truck burst into a conspiratorial buzz)

ANNA. Chush!

(They stop instantly, eyeing her)

*(Clump of bushes: TURK, THORPE, DOOLAN, WILLY and BECK peer through the scrub down to the tiny inlet below)

DOOLAN. Eyoop, watch it.

(They peer at something on the water that can't be made out at first in the darkness)

THORPE. Is it?

BECK. Yea.

TURK. Eh? -

DOOLAN. Boat!

TURK. - can't see...

DOOLAN. By the light there, little light, see?

(They peer at the inlet: the dark outline of a boat can be seen, with a dim light burning)

WILLY. Trawler.

DOOLAN. No, not like that, never a trawler like that.

BECK. Military, is it? - no guns.

(THORPE is focussing a fieldglass on it)

WILLY. Mm.

TURK. Dead peculiar, intit? All that junk on it!

DOOLAN. Like one of those old pleasure boats, you know, day at sea or trips round the bay, with bits stuck on -

WILLY. It'll have wireless though.

DOOLAN. (a flat statement) - any more for the Skylark.

(Pause)

TURK. Dead quiet, anyrate.

WILLY. Yes.

TURK. No-one about.

THORPE. (cautious) Not that you can see.

DOOLAN. Where's the crew, then?

(Pause)

WILLY. Could it be something to do with... y'know, us?

THORPE. MHQ?

WILLY. Yes?

(Pause)

DOOLAN. Well...

THORPE. They wouldn't leave a light on, would they?

BECK. Anyhow, it was the morning, wasn't it? - they were supposed to arrive.

WILLY. Aye, but in a boat, just like that. That's what I heard. Just to act as HQ, wireless post - nothing combatant.

THORPE. And they swop their plans round so often.

(Pause)

DOOLAN. Could be something then?

WILLY. Of theirs?

DOOLAN. Well...

THORPE. We don't <u>know</u>, do we?

    (Pause)

TURK. We'd better find out then, hadn't we.

THORPE. How?

TURK. Like this, look. Hup!

    (He jumps up, and starts leaping down the hillside. They shout at him: BECK and WILLY try to stop him)

  *(Inside lorry. They hear the noise. ANNA sticks her head through the canvas back of the lorry)

ANNA. What is it? (no reply) Eh?

   *(Clump of bushes. DOOLAN hisses her and waves her down)

   *(Inside lorry. She turns back in)

RAPS. Well?

ANNA. (burning) I don't know, do I?

AJUS II. (Malay to the OLD WOMAN, quite loudly)

ANNA. Shut up.

  * (Clump of bushes)

DOOLAN. Maniac, look at him.

THORPE. Proving his point anyhow.

DOOLAN. He's what?

THORPE. Well, no-one's firing.

DOOLAN. Probably watching him entranced.

       *(TURK springs down the hillside. BECK and WILLY follow, making an attempt to keep covered and trying to stop him)

TURK. (as he jumps) Hey - hup - oops -

*(Clump of bushes)

THORPE. You wonder why he's here.

DOOLAN. Eh?

THORPE. You wonder if he understands the principles involved, what we're all fighting for.

DOOLAN. Oh, that, yes.

*(Inside lorry)

AJUS. It is time, only, er - an hour?

RAPS. Eh?

AJUS. - before Imperial Army...

RAPS. Right on our tail, shouldn't wonder.

AJUS. I listen.

(The OLD MAN on the floor groans. GRAN turns on ANNA and RAPS and shouts angrily at them in Malay)

ANNA. For God's sake -

*(Clump of bushes)

DOOLAN. (hearing this) Let's let off a rocket, let everyone know we're here.

THORPE. He's there.

DOOLAN. (peering) Yes?

*(In the lorry, GRAN gets even louder)

DOOLAN. (hissing) Quiet!

*(The beach. TURK tumbles the last few feet and stops abruptly right on the water's edge)

TURK. (points, panting) Ha!

(The other two join him: they still have their weapons:
TURK has discarded his)

BECK.   For Chrissake!

TURK.   Look - see them?

BECK.   - you stupid... you could have done for us if there was
anyone on board!

TURK.   There wasn't though, was there?

WILLY.   Dinghies!

TURK.   Aye, two of them. Well, there you are then, all laid on
waiting. And there's another further up - they come ashore
for a bit of whoopee, there's no-one there, there can't be!

WILLY.   What about below decks? -

TURK.   For chrissake -

WILLY.   You don't just leave a boat without -

TURK.   (cups his hands to his mouth and shouts) Is there
anyone below decks?

(WILLY and BECK speechless: silence from the boat)

TURK.   (turning back to them) There you are see?

(Clump of bushes. DOOLAN and THORPE, eyes screwed up
tight, gritting teeth.

Inside lorry. An islander says something in Malay. Some
nod, but GRANNY replies sharply./ Several islanders talk
in Malay, quietly./ RAPS, lighting a cigarette, watches.

The beach. WILLY, BECK and TURK push off dinghy from
the shore.

Clump of bushes. DOOLAN sees them and points./ THORPE
looks through eyeglass./ His point of view: they paddle forward
on the dark water.

Boat deck. Pan across deserted deck./ WILLY, BECK and
TURK appear over the side stealthily - via a scramblenet -
a tiny light burns over a ramshackle wheelhouse at the stern.

114

Inside lorry. The islanders, sweating, preparing to run./
RAPS eases himself quietly out of the way.

Boat deck. WILLY suddenly stops and points./ A man lies
on his face on a mattress near the wheelhouse.

Inside lorry. Several islanders suddenly get up and jump
out./ ANNA and GRAN yell at them./ RAPS hides.

Bushes. DOOLAN and THORPE react.

Boat deck. BECK and WILLY react and take cover by the
companion hatch. /TURK only half-hides, grinning)

WILLY. (to him) Down!

    *(By the lorry. GRAN bellows after the fleeing locals, pulls
    up stones and earth and hurls after them)

THORPE. Stop her for God's sake, shut her up!

    *(Boat deck. TURK chuckles out loud)

DOOLAN. (in bushes) Hey! (He pulls up stones and starts to
    throw them at GRAN) - Stop that!

    (By the lorry. GRAN turns and starts throwing stones at
    him. ANNA grapples with her trying to drag her back in.

Boat deck. TURK, chuckling, scampers across the deck
and disappears: the other two hiss after him, trying to
stop him.

Inside lorry. THORPE, DOOLAN and ANNA are bundling
GRAN in, and shout over the racket. Two other Malays
are still in the lorry, and shouting too)

DOOLAN. Rappers!

RAPS. Hallo.

DOOLAN. Move this thing. Down there.

THORPE. With the boat there?

DOOLAN. - an aunt sally! - on the hill here.

   *(Boat deck)

WILLY. Here they come.

BECK. Where's he gone?

WILLY. Mm? Oh - (shrugs)

BECK. (swears)

WILLY. What about...? (he gestures towards the wheelhouse)

   (They raise themselves cautiously and peer)

BECK. Hasn't moved.

   (They cautiously cross the deck and stand over him. / THE
   MAN breathes wheezily. WILLY points to several bottles
   nearby)

BECK. (nods) Phew! (pushes figure with foot) Hey! Hey you.
Wake up. Hey!

MAN. (mumbles incoherently)

   (BECK turns him over with his foot. / THE MAN is dressed
   in an ancient but once ornate captain's uniform. He is very
   gaunt and wears elaborate whiskers on his bony face and a
   thick green eyeshade on his forehead, giving him a
   spectacularly sinister appearance)

BECK. Ch! You alone, eh? Alone? Other people here?
Speakee English? Wake up you ugly sod -

   (He kicks him. THE CAPTAIN mutters incomprehensibly,
   half-opening his eyes)

WILLY. (on his haunches, close to him) Wireless? Do you
have a wireless?

   (CAPTAIN subsides)

BECK. Ach, useless.

WILLY. I'll look below.

*(Truck arrives at the waterside. Inside it -)

DOOLAN. (indicating arms, ammunition and explosives) Leave all that stuff.

THORPE. Leave it?

DOOLAN. Get it later.

(They spill out and make for the second dinghy.

Inside the boat - corridor. WILLY runs along the cramped corridor, off which are four small doors. A dim light burns in the ceiling. He finds the wireless equipment in a little alcove in the crewroom.

Boat deck. THORPE appears over the side, stopping dead when he sees BECK and the DRUNK)

BECK. We think it's the Captain.

THORPE. Oh yes?

BECK. He's pissed.

THORPE. Willy?

BECK. Below looking for the transmitter.

RAPS. (arriving over the side) Where's laughing boy?

BECK. You got the gear in that boat?

RAPS. Eh?

BECK. Firearms, ammo, all the stuff -

THORPE. Er, we'll get it later.

BECK. What?

THORPE. In the lorry. Must get the injured up first...

BECK. (incredulous) !

DOOLAN. (arriving) Heh! Move!

(THORPE and RAPS make for the companionway. In the

background, the two injured are brought aboard)

BECK. Sunday School outing!

   *(Corridor. RAPS enters galley and THORPE the crewroom./
   ANNA and GRAN carry the GIRL and assist AJUS II down the
   companion ladder.

   *Galley. RAPS is investigating. He opens several food
   containers)

RAPS. Rice. (he opens another) Rice. (he opens another)
   Rice.

   (Spots cupboard, opens it hopefully. It is full of tins)

   Ah! (he gets one down and reads the label) Rice pudding.

   *(Crewroom. They examine the wireless equipment)

THORPE. Is it...?

WILLY. It'll take a time.

THORPE. How long?

WILLY. ...half an hour.

THORPE. Mm. Er - Turk?

WILLY. (shrugs)

   (In background, GRAN has placed GIRL on a bunk: she helps
   ANNA with AJUS II)

ANNA. Can you...?

   (THORPE helps. They lay him on a bunk, injured and in
   great pain.)

   *(Deck. BECK and RAPS huddled in a nook behind the
   wheelhouse, eating rice putting out of tins with a spoon)

BECK. This no-one-in-charge business, all pals together, it's
   stupid. My last job, this RSM was a bastard, a real bastard,
   kept order with his boots and a pickhandle.

RAPS. That's it, yes, a man's life.

118

BECK. Worked a treat.

RAPS. It would do, obviously.

   *(Crewroom. ANNA cuts bloodied wrappings from AJUS'
   chest: white bone fragments protrude)

  *(Deck. AJUS listening. THORPE appears at the top of
  companion ladder)

DOOLAN. Beck.

BECK. Wait.

AJUS. Chushush!

DOOLAN. Eh?

AJUS. Truck.

DOOLAN.. I can't -

THORPE. Listen!

   (Pause)

AJUS. There.

THORPE. (shakes head)

DOOLAN. How far?

AJUS. Close.

DOOLAN. (he indicates to BECK to douse the light) - Heh!
   (BECK does so)

   (Pause)

THORPE. What, erm, what do we do?

DOOLAN. Sit quiet and hope.

RAPS. They'll see the truck, look -

THORPE. No -

RAPS. They will, look it's -

BECK. That rock see?

RAPS. Rock?

BECK. Hides it, they might not see it from up there.

  (Pause. No-one moves)

DOOLAN. (uncertain) Could be the crew coming back.

RAPS. Could be, yes.

THORPE. And if it's not?

  (Pause)

DOOLAN. We could, er -

RAPS. What?

BECK. ...push off a bit.

AJUS. Ayeh.

  (Pause)

THORPE. In this?

BECK. Well -

DOOLAN. Just out of range?

THORPE. If you, er -

RAPS. I mean...

  (Pause. None of them really believes this to be feasible, but
  to oppose it would be to take on individual responsibility)

DOOLAN. I'll go and see if Willy can - make this thing go then,
  shall I?

  (He doesn't move)

THORPE. There must be an engine somewhere.

RAPS. Must be, yes.

  (DOOLAN goes)

120

RAPS. All for the best, I expect.

(THE CAPTAIN mutters incomprehensibly)

AJUS (suddenly) Eh!

(The truck can be heard approaching very faintly)

*(Engineroom. WILLY runs in followed by DOOLAN. They look at the engine, a very rickety affair)

WILLY. Hmm!

(He sets to work)

*(Deck. BECK hauls THE CAPTAIN into the wheelhouse)

BECK. Get in there! Get in!

(THORPE and RAPS rapidly bring up material from the dinghy: they clear the deck of any signs of their presence.

Corridor. AJUS runs along, hissing for silence from engineroom and crewroom.

Deck. THORPE suddenly waves the other to get down. He points. We see their viewpoint: the brow of the hill. A truck gently eases into position, just visible in the darkness)

(Deck-wheelhouse. BECK pushes CAPTAIN down to a sitting position, and bangs on the deck with his fist)

*(Engineroom)

WILLY. (whisper) It runs on paraffin!

(DOOLAN listening)

WILLY. There's plenty here.

DOOLAN. Shush!

*(Crewroom. ANNA and GRAN hold still, listening)

GRAN. (Malay, sharply, to ANNA)

ANNA. Shush!

(On deck)

RAPS. They must see the wagon, they must.

(They watch, dead still.

The enemy truck. Silence, not a movement)

THORPE. (on deck) They're not sure.

(Pause)

BECK. It's a big truck.

AJUS. Ayeh.

BECK. Maybe - twelve of them.

THORPE. Looking for us.

(Pause)

CAPTAIN. (suddenly splutters)

(BECK grasps him and puts his hand over his mouth. They
look at the truck - silence.

Engineroom. DOOLAN and WILLY, listening. Faint taps
on the hull, maybe a piece of wood knocking against the side
with the swell)

(Deck)

THORPE. (between teeth) Go away, go away...

TURK. (shout from the darkness) - Hey!

THORPE. Christ!

TURK. Hey where are you, what you done with the dinghy?

THORPE. (as loud as he dares) Shut up and get down!

TURK. What?

(Distant shouts in Malay and immediate burst of tommygun
fire. Bullets strike the metal deck and ricochet)

BECK. Right, that's it then.

THORPE. (shouts) Start her, start her up!

BECK. (bangs on deck) Right, come on then! Boat move, eh? Come on, you sod, savvy, move it! (hits CAPTAIN with rifle butt) Move!

(Engineroom. WILLY and DOOLAN. The engine roars into life first time.

TURK races along the water's edge and dives in. Bullets strike around him.

Crewroom. The porthole glass is shattered. GRAN tries to protect the CHILD.

Deck. THORPE releases the anchor chain, which runs through with a roar.

Engineroom. The engine pounds up to a high pitch.

Crewroom. AJUS II is in agony with the vibrations.

Deck - wheelhouse. CAPTAIN operates the primitive controls and shouts something at BECK. Glass shatters around them and BECK drops for cover. The boat starts to move.

The enemy truck. Flashes of smallarms and automatic weapons. / Longshot of their point of view - the dark shape of the boat moving. / Close shot of the threshed-up water at the stern as the boat lumbers into motion: pan along to - close shot TURK in the water, swimming strongly.

Corridor. GRAN runs out of the crewroom with GIRL in her arms and crouches down in the corridor with her for protection.

*Deck. RAPS spots something on shore. He points)

RAPS. Hey! -

*(Engineroom)

WILLY. (shouts over noise) I don't know how - but it works!

DOOLAN. (thumbs up: runs out)

123

*(Deck: wheelhouse)

RAPS. (shouts) The truck, look!

BECK. Eh?

RAPS. (points)

(Their viewpoint: the truck they arrived in is on fire)

*(Deck - wheelhouse)

THORPE. (staring at it) Turk!

BECK. Maniac.

THORPE. Where... What is he...?

RAPS. Turk!

BECK. Leave him.

THORPE. All the ammunition and everything, it's...

BECK. Leave him! Come on, move it!

(He opens the throttle full: the boat vibrates and moves.

Crewroom: AJUS II coughing and in agony from the heavy
vibration.

Close shot TURK grasping the bottom of the scramble net and
heaving himself clear of the water. Burst of fire and he is hit.
He falls upside down, his legs entangled in the netting, half in
the water. The boat is moving)

(Deck - wheelhouse)

BECK. (yells at CAPTAIN) Come on! Come on!

THORPE. (pointing) Look!

(The lorry explodes, scattering burning debris in every
direction)

(Deck: top of companion ladder)

DOOLAN. Great one for the big gestures, Turk. (gunfire)
Should have run a circus.

124

(Crewroom. The whole structure judders appallingly.
AJUS II lies still: ANNA sees that he is dead.

Wide shot of valley. The lorry burns fiercely: flashing
from guns nearby. Debris scattered by the explosion has
started numerous small fires around, filling the valley with
the dull red light of flame./ The movement of the boat has
hauled up the scramblenet automatically, pivoting on the
yardcrane, so TURK's inert body swings in a huge arc
across the deck, upside down and high above the wheelhouse.
It is seen to judder from the impact of more bullets as it
hangs there. The boat moves out into the darkness: guns
blaze after it.

Fade)

(Fade up. Crewroom./Night./Deep steady throb of engine.
WILLY works at the wireless equipment by the light of a pocket
torch. ANNA attends to TURK who is unconscious. GRAN
sits over the GIRL. The rest are asleep./ Distant thump of
guns./TURK comes round, and screws up his face in
agony)

ANNA. Stay still.

TURK. What...?

ANNA. You got shot up.

TURK. Bad?

ANNA. Yes.

TURK. Where?

ANNA. Shoulder, thigh, belly.

TURK. Huh. I did it properly then.

(He feels the boat's movements)

On a little trip, are we? (no reply) How long we been
going?

WILLY. Keep it down, can't you?

TURK. That's Willy.

WILLY. Let them sleep- and I'm trying to fix this, trying to listen.

TURK. Fix what? (no reply) Fix what?

ANNA. Radio.

TURK. How long we been going? (no reply) Eh?

(Silence. BECK mumbles in his sleep. Distant thump of guns on the mainland)

DOOLAN. (lying awake in the dark) Listen to them, eh? Big ones those.

TURK. How long?

ANNA. I don't know.

TURK. Well, hours or -

ANNA. I don't know!

DOOLAN. Shut it, can't you?

WILLY. When you've a minute...

ANNA. Mm?

WILLY. - hold this a minute.

ANNA. (rises and crosses to him)

WILLY. Like that, shine it there.

ANNA. (does so)

TURK. I thought you were fixing my shoulder or something?

(GRAN says something in Malay to the unconscious GIRL, a rising inflection. She turns to WILLY and ANNA and repeats it to them, searching their faces for comment)

(DOOLAN heaves himself off his bunk)

TURK. Doolan?

(He goes out)

(faint) The water, last thing that I... what's the matter,
I'm as weak as a chick.

WILLY. (re the torch) More round here, that's it.

(TURK feels for the position of his wounds with his free
hand. Darkness still. Thump of guns.

The dark shape of the mainland. The flashes of guns can
be seen several miles away, and the glow of a bushfire)

*(Deck - wheelhouse. THORPE is slumped forward, gun over
his lap. THE CAPTAIN is sitting at the wheel, still pretty
incapable)

DOOLAN. (arriving) Eh.

THORPE. (straightening) I'm not asleep.

DOOLAN. I'll take over for a bit.

THORPE. Plane, listen. (he gestures to the sky)

(They hear it droning around)

DOOLAN. He been alright?

THORPE. Mm? (DOOLAN indicates CAPTAIN) Oh yes. (looks
up) It's looking for us.

(Pause)

DOOLAN. You'd better get some kip.

THORPE. I'm alright.

DOOLAN. You don't look it.

THORPE. I must just get through this.

DOOLAN. Through what?

(Pause)

THORPE. (shakes his head groggily) What happened, what went
wrong?

DOOLAN. Back there?

THORPE. The whole operation. It was all worked out, it was on paper, should have just clicked into place.

DOOLAN. Ah well, it didn't. Nor's your -

THORPE. Mm?

DOOLAN. ... no-one-in-charge business. There's got to be someone -

THORPE. It'll work.

DOOLAN. - you know, to hold it together.

(Gunfire: DOOLAN looks at the mainland)

Look at that. Fifty-pounders they'd be.

THORPE. We stuck exactly to plan -

DOOLAN. Ach, poor bastards.

THORPE. Mm?

DOOLAN. Any blokes caught up in that lot.

*(Crewroom)

WILLY. He's out.

ANNA. Wh -?

WILLY. Turk.

ANNA. (barely a glance) Yes.

(Pause)

(outburst) What was he doing? - do you know?

WILLY. Which particular time?

ANNA. The lorry, blowing up the lorry, and -

WILLY. Burning his boats I think.

ANNA. He what?

WILLY. And ours. So he couldn't go back even if he wanted.

128

Nor us. So we had to go.

ANNA. But - why involve all of us in what he...?

WILLY. (shrugs)

ANNA. What? Is there only him in the world? I feel sick at it,
sick!

(Pause)

You know that boy that was injured here, the one who - we
put over, you know he'd be alive now, don't you, if he
hadn't... It's all a big joke to him isn't it? - he doesn't
care what happens, not really, never has done, he's just in
it for kicks. Beck and Doolan they're maybe only here
for the money but at least they're sort of professional
about it, they don't - (gunfire) Ach, listen, listen to it; it
makes me sick to have to touch him.

WILLY. (moving torch) That's it.

ANNA. Why couldn't they have left him strung up there,
that's what should have happened... risk getting
killed just to get him down. Let him get himself shot up,
but leave us out of it, we're not... risking the whole
venture and what we could do if only... listen, listen to it.

(She wipes her hands clean on her clothing. GRAN talks to
the LITTLE GIRL in Malay)

When we go back, though, we might get somewhere.

RAPS. How do you mean?

ANNA. Well, he can't move. If he's still alive he'll have to stay
on board here.

RAPS. You mean, if we go back there?

ANNA. (surprise that he is surprised) Yes!

(Gunfire. GRAN talks to the LITTLE GIRL)

WILLY. What about her?

ANNA. Mm?

WILLY. What's wrong with... (gestures at the GIRL)

ANNA. I don't know. It's a surface wound, a lot of blood but -

WILLY. She thinks it's more than that.

ANNA. How can you...?

WILLY. (indicates 'listen')

(GRAN is stroking the GIRL's forehead, half-talking, half-singing to her very quietly)

*(Deck)

DOOLAN. See those little gold sparks flashing down there, see them? That's a three-oh-three rattler, can kill 170 a minute. And look, over there, looks like the whole countryside's on fire right across? It's the singers - you know, flamethrowers - that do that. They use them to flush out any troops hidden in the bush, but there's usually the locals hiding there too, women, kids, all of them. I've done it. Little kids running around and screaming with their clothes all on fire. We used to try and make it quicker for them, but if you were short of ammo, well... (he shrugs)

THORPE. Why?

DOOLAN. Why what?

THORPE. Why the kids for godsake?

DOOLAN. Oh - (slow) - it's always the kids, it's always the kids.

(Gunfire)

DOOLAN. Turk's round.

THORPE. Yes?

DOOLAN. What - er -

THORPE. Eh?

DOOLAN. What do we do if we can't fix the radio?

THORPE. Oh, er, ... (screws up his eyes) - can't think at the moment.

(The plane is heard, droning around overhead,

130

DOOLAN looks up at it)

DOOLAN. You got kids then?

THORPE. I've got a son, yes.

DOOLAN. Where's he now?

THORPE. I don't know. With his mother somewhere. He'd be seven now.

DOOLAN. Married were you?

THORPE. Oh yes.

DOOLAN. What happened?

THORPE. Oh - (shrugs) - you know.

DOOLAN. Ah.

THORPE. You?

DOOLAN. (beat) No kids.

*(Crewroom)

BECK. (lying in the dark) There's that plane.

TURK. Awake are you Beck?

BECK. Listen to it.

(It is heard droning around overhead, looking for them)

RAPS. It won't see us in the dark.

AJUS. (moans quietly in Malay)

BECK. (quietly) Belt up.

AJUS. Is my village. On fire, look, the sky.

BECK. You can't tell what village that is!

AJUS. (Malay)

RAPS. Maybe his wife and kids are there.

BECK. He's lucky then, isn't he?

TURK. That's a stupid bleeding thing to say.

BECK. Listen you, shut it, you've done enough.

TURK. I what? What's the matter with you?

ANNA. He shouldn't have had kids. Not with...

TURK. With what? What are you talking about?

ANNA. All this, you know - (gestures)

(Gunfire)

TURK. But he couldn't have known! -

ANNA. - listen to it, listen -

TURK. No, could he? I mean, how could he? - when he had
the kids; that this was going to happen!

ANNA. (outburst) No-one should have kids, not now, it's...
not now, not with the world going the way it is, people...
(gesture) - no-one should have kids.

TURK. You what? Eh?

(The plane is heard overhead)

RAPS. (lying in the dark, listening) Like the blitz again,
isn't it? In the cupboard under the stairs listening for the

132

bombs to start, with my little sister.

(Gunfire. AJUS moans high in Malay)

WILLY. Why don't you get some sleep while you can?

(They lie awake in the dark, eyes wide open, listening. GRAN
strokes the GIRL's forehead, crooning gently to her.
Gunfire)

*(Deck. THORPE has fallen asleep. He slowly slips
down the post he is leaning against; then wakes and jerks
himself upright)

DOOLAN. For chrissake.

THORPE. I'm alright.

(CAPTAIN approaches with papers, saying something
incomprehensible)

DOOLAN. Right, Sinbad, watch it.

CAPTAIN. (indicates papers, and explains them)

THORPE. It's a map, look.

DOOLAN. What's he saying? What you want, eh?

(CAPTAIN blearily points to the horizon then to the map)

DOOLAN. There's a little light there, look, flashing. Long way
off. Some sort of market buoy, or a lighthouse even. (He
takes map) Glasgow?

(CAPTAIN again indicates the light then a spot on the top
chart just off Glasgow)

DOOLAN. Did you find out what he's been drinking?

THORPE. There's a crate of it here.

DOOLAN. (smelling it) Phew. (to CAPTAIN) Get back in there,
Romeo, just keep this thing going in a straight line OK? -
leave the fancy navigation to us, I don't think it's your
forte. (CAPTAIN goes back) Evil looking bastard, isn't
he?

THORPE. Ayeh.

DOOLAN. Win a competition.

(THE CAPTAIN, sensing they are discussing him, glares blearily at them)

What is this bloody boat, eh? Cargo? Fishing? What's it for, this boat? Dead peculiar.

(CAPTAIN shrugs and gestures)

Forget it. Let's have a look at these, eh? See which way we're going, make some sense out of them.

(He spreads out the charts. THORPE has fallen asleep again)

Just keep straight on, OK? (he points - this way.
Away from all that.

(He thumbs at the burning mainland, and studies the charts./ We see the distant mainland, lighting up the sky./ The plane drones close. Fade)

(Fade up. Crewroom, 3 a.m. WILLY slumped asleep over the wireless desk./ The others asleep on the floor or on bunks, except for ANNA, who doggedly works at an old first-aid chest she has found./ The regular sway of the boat)

(On deck there is a sudden shout and two rifle shots: then a pitch and lurch of the boat./ BECK and WILLY stumble up and out: they mount the companion ladder)

RAPS. (waking) What was it? What was that?

(GRAN shouts at him and AJUS, who scurry out after the other two.

*Deck - top of companion ladder. WILLY and BECK emerge cautiously, keeping under cover. It is now quite black: the glow in the sky has gone)

BECK. (quietly) Hey. (silence) What goes on? (silence) Doolan?

(Rapidly:)

DOOLAN. Stay low.

134

WILLY. You all right?

DOOLAN. Bit of a scratch, nothing much.

WILLY. Thorpe?

THORPE. (quietly) I'm here.

DOOLAN. Did he clip you?

THORPE. No.

BECK. Eh?

DOOLAN. It's Captain Cook there. Suddenly grabs the gun.

BECK. He what?

THORPE. I must have been asleep.

BECK. He got your firearm from you?

    (There is a shot, striking close to BECK. They duck)

  *(Crewroom. TURK is sitting, half-up)

TURK. I can't just lie here and... (to ANNA) Hey -

ANNA. Don't talk to me.

TURK. But I can't just... (he shouts) Doolan!

    (The boat lurches again, throwing TURK on his injured
    shoulder against the bunkhead. He shouts in great pain)

  *(Deck. THE CAPTAIN suddenly shouts out something in his
  own language. The boat lurches)

(BECK. What's he doing? (shouts) What's he doing?   )
(   )   o
(DOOLAN. Watch it.   )   v
(   )   e
(BECK. Is it deliberate, or -   )   r
(   )   l
(THORPE. He's pretty drunk still.   )   a
(   )   p
(WILLY. Perhaps he's just lurching about -   )   p
(   )   ing

135

(DOOLAN. - his aim's all over the place.   )
(   )
(WILLY. - could be sort of falling against the wheel or)
(something.   )

THORPE. No, it's more definite than that.

AJUS. Ayeh.

THORPE. He's up to something.

    (Pause)

BECK. Pa! (raises rifle)

(WILLY. No - Beck -   )
(   )
(DOOLAN. What is it?   )
(   )
(THORPE. Stop him.   )
(   ) overlapping
(WILLY. I am.   )
(   )
(BECK. Eh?   )
(   )
(WILLY. That won't solve anything.   )
(   )
(BECK. You what?   )

THORPE. Wait till he runs out of ammunition, then rush him.
    No risks, eh? - there's no point.

RAPS. Yes.

BECK. What do you mean? - I could do for him, just like that.

THORPE. (authoritatively) I'm sure you could, but you're
    not going to, alright?

BECK. You going to stop me?

THORPE. If necessary.

BECK. Yea?

    (DOOLAN delighted. There is a rapid, businesslike
    atmosphere)

WILLY. How much's he got?

136

DOOLAN. Ammo? (to THORPE) Was it a full mag?

THORPE. I think so.

BECK. Think so!

DOOLAN. Two down then, four to go.

THORPE. Three down.

DOOLAN. Eh?

THORPE. Three, there's been three shots.

RAPS. (uncertain) We wait then.

THORPE. (very positive) Yes.

(Pause)

DOOLAN. Beck.

BECK. Ach (lowers gun)

*(Crewroom. TURK comes round: he is in appalling pain. ANNA is changing his shoulder dressing)

TURK. (whispering) Can't you give me anything to stop the - y'know...

ANNA. No.

TURK. But you must have got -

ANNA. You destroyed it all.

TURK. Heh?

ANNA. All the medical supplies were in that lorry, with everything else.

(Pause. He absorbs this: then jerks with sudden pain as she removes a dressing)

TURK. How deep is that? (the wound) Is it still in there?

ANNA. What?

TURK. Bullet, shrapnel, whatever it is.

ANNA. (shrugs)

TURK. Eh? It could poison me if it is, could get into my
bloodstream. It didn't go right through, then?

ANNA. I don't know.

TURK. (with mounting alarm) But you've looked.

ANNA. Looked?

TURK. Yes, looked, on me other side, see if there's a hole
it come out of. It's a flesh wound, intit?

ANNA. No, I haven't looked.

TURK. Well, bloody look now!

ANNA. (looks) Nothing.

(She continues: TURK fidgets and frets)

TURK. I feel hot, I must have a fever, I've a fever, cover me up.
It's blood poisoning, it's got into my... Have you got a
watch? (feels pulse) Feels pretty fast to me, I wonder
if... (he feels) Feels pretty fast to me.

ANNA. (amused in spite of herself) Good.

TURK. Eh? Fine bloody nurse you are, great comfort. (he
frets) If I was up there...

ANNA. You can't do anything.

TURK. I know that, don't I? - I'm well aware of that. Stuck
down here like an old parrot in a cage, going mad.

* (Deck)

AJUS. Heh. (he points)

(Wheelhouse. CAPTAIN moves unsteadily to the far end:
his head and shoulders can still be seen)

THORPE. Where's he going?

DOOLAN. To have a quiet pee I should think.

BECK. (slaps his rifle butt meditatively)

RAPS. I couldn't, not with five people watching.

(Pause)

WILLY. I'll get back to it then.

THORPE. Right.

(WILLY goes below)

RAPS. Getting cold.

DOOLAN. Chuck us over a dressing or something.

RAPS. Got you, did he?

DOOLAN. Only a scratch.

RAPS. Here.

(He throws a dressing. It falls short. They look at it and towards the wheelhouse./AJUS darts across, picks it up and is behind the bollard sheltering DOOLAN before the shot comes: it is wide)

THORPE. Four down.

DOOLAN. (unwrapping the dressing) He'll have to do better than that, even halfway through a pee.

BECK. I could just clip him -

RAPS. - er -

BECK. - he'd come to heel then.

THORPE. (hard) I shouldn't.

BECK. Who's to stop me?

(Silence)

*(Crewroom. WILLY is crossing to the radio equipment)

TURK. (very weak) Why can't you do for him then?

WILLY. There's no point. This - (wireless equipment) - is

139

what matters.

TURK. (almost inaudible) That! I don't believe that's ever bloody worked.

(ANNA watches him as she works: it is the first time she has really looked at him)

ANNA. You've no resistance, have you? - all skin and bone.

TURK. Yea?

ANNA. Don't you eat?

TURK. Yes I eat, of course I eat.

(Pause. She works)

ANNA. How long have you been living like this?

TURK. Since I got out the regulars. Ten years.

ANNA. As a mercenary.

TURK. Five years Israel, two Algeria. The rest all over.

ANNA. For nothing, though.

TURK. Eh?

ANNA. No... purpose to it.

TURK. What do you mean? - it's me, innit, it's what I do!

ANNA. - alright.

TURK. I mean, used to. (beat) What do you mean, "purpose", I didn't just... I was doing something, not just carrying on like a - like a...

ANNA. Easy, alright -

TURK. (stung) I bet you stood up for every Righteous Cause in the Book, one of Nature's bloody martyrs! -

ANNA. (calm) There's a lot to be done.

TURK. I know, I know that!

(They fall silent, full of resentment for each other.)

*(Deck. Pan along the row of besiegers, watching. Silence)

DOOLAN. It's a long pee.

RAPS. It is, isn't it?

(Pause)

Maybe that's what he was trying to tell us, he was bursting
to go. That's why he took over, it was that or burst.

(Pause)

DOOLAN. Then why did he show us Glasgow on the map?

(Pause)

RAPS. Maybe that's where he was last time he went.

AJUS. He's move now.

(BECK raises gun)

THORPE. (looks across at him)

BECK. (senses look and returns it defiantly)

THORPE. (holds look on him)

BECK. (bangs his gun down)

(Wheelhouse. CAPTAIN crosses back to his original
position, but is now masked from them by some deck
structures. It is very shadowy and difficult to see.

AJUS. (points to sky) Daylight one hour.

DOOLAN. Have to do something by then Mr. Thorpe.

BECK. Never left home before, telling soldiers what to do -

RAPS. Eh?

BECK. - one of these cunt eggheads, got it all from books.

RAPS. Thorpe?

BECK. Eh?

RAPS. Thorpe.

BECK. I'm better than him.

   (Pause)

   I got medals, ent I? - what's he got? - exams or something?
   - not even a soldier. Korea I done and Cyprus and Malaya
   and places he ent even heard of... I'm better than him!

AJUS. Cold.

DOOLAN. Yip. Clouds coming up.

THORPE. Is he still there?

DOOLAN. I think so. You can't tell too clearly, all that
   shadow. There - he's moving, see?

   (Pause)

THORPE. He's altered course you know.

DOOLAN. Yea?

THORPE. The stars, I've been working it out. He's taking us
   much more to the south.

DOOLAN. There's nothing to the south, just an awful lot of sea.

THORPE. (thoughtful) Yes.

   (Huge sea-scape, still and empty: first signs of dawn)

THORPE. Perhaps I shouldn't have stopped him. (looks at
   wheelhouse) - he's up to something. It might have been
   better to...

DOOLAN. (looks at him)

THORPE. After all, we've no control as it is, and... can't

142

tell, he may be right. What do you think? I'm... not sure.

(He shivers and draws his clothes tighter around him)

Cold.

AJUS. (sharp) There, look, again.

THORPE. (looking) No.

AJUS. Is very difficult to see. Like goost.

DOOLAN. Like what?

AJUS. Goost.

DOOLAN. Oh ghost!

AJUS. (nodding) Dead person.

(Wheelhouse. Shadowy movements)

THORPE. (full retreat) Anyhow, we're all in this.

(The engine, which has been throbbing away regularly, starts to beat jerkily)

Listen.

(It stops: the flywheel starts to run down with a dull whine)

The engine.

(They listen)

BECK. It's stopped.

(RAPS starts to descend the companion ladder)

*Crewroom. WILLY leaves the radio and crosses to the corridor)

GRAN. (Malay: What has happened, what's that noise?)

143

(Close shot TURK, listening)

*(Corridor. RAPS and WILLY meet)

RAPS. What is it?

(They enter the engineroom.)

*(Deck)

DOOLAN. There's plenty of fuel.

THORPE. Could he have done it?

(They look across.)

*(Crewroom. The whine-down of the flywheel stops: silence)

TURK. (shouts) What's going on?

*(Engineroom. WILLY examines the engine: silence.

*Deck. Pan across the quiet deck)

AJUS. (points to sky) Look.

(First signs of dawn in the cloudy sky.

BECK lights a cigarette and draws his clothes tighter round
him)

BECK. Cold.

DOOLAN. Ayeh.

BECK. Oh for a little transistor.

THORPE. Listen.

(They do)

DOOLAN. What?

THORPE. The quiet.

(The whole ocean is still. There comes a dull hammering

144

from the engineroom below, echoing across the water)

AJUS. (in admiration) Look! Look!

(They look at the cloudy dawn)

BECK. Plane'll find us now, for sure.

DOOLAN. How far have we come, you reckon?

THORPE. Oh - (shrugs)

(Silence.)

(Suddenly, from the west, there is a great flare of whitish-
yellow light, flooding the entire sky with an immense and
dazzling brilliance. After a few seconds it changes to
yellow-red, then orange-red: then an immense ball of fire,
probably fifty miles across, looms and rolls into existence.
The blaze of light begins to fade sharply: and darkness
starts to fall again./ It is incredibly beautiful: it lasts in
all some 20 - 30 seconds, and is accompanied by complete
silence and stillness. It is as though the sun has suddenly
sprung up to give instant, dazzling, hot day: and then
dropped back again, as abruptly, below the horizon, producing
darkness and 5 a.m. chill once more.

Deck. All except AJUS instinctively throw themselves down
flat.

Engineroom. RAPS and WILLY run to the outer wall as the
light streams through the porthole.

Deck. AJUS stands as if hypnotised by the sight: he shouts -)

AJUS. (at the top of his voice) Pika-don!

  *(Crewroom)

(GRAN. (shriek) Stand by da! Stand by da!   )
(   ) sim.
(TURK. It's a searchlight, move us away from the)
(window, quick, quick, move us!   )

  *(Deck)

AJUS. Pika-don!

DOOLAN. What's he saying?

145

THORPE. (to AJUS) No!

AJUS. Pika-don!

DOOLAN. What's he saying?

THORPE. Atombomb.

(They stare at it)

BECK. (quiet) Christ.

DOOLAN. What - is it then?

(Pause. The most uncanny thing is the complete silence)

A volcano, is it, erupting or something?

BECK. How do you know it's not...

THORPE. The cloud would be mushroom-shaped. This isn't.

AJUS. (shouts high up in Malay)

(The phenomenon is reaching a colossal height, swirling and billowing black smoke dominating the entire sky.

(RAPS and WILLY run out of the companion hatch and stop dead when they see it. They stare at it)

RAPS. (quiet) God god god.

DOOLAN. (quiet) Like the end of the world.

*(Crewroom. ANNA and GRAN stare transfixed at the sight)

GIRL. (in Malay: What is it? What is it?)

*(Deck)

THORPE. North-west, about.

WILLY. How far?

THORPE. Oh - (shakes head)

DOOLAN. The Yanks do test-things over that way.

146

THORPE. What.

DOOLAN. Oh, bombs and things, they test them.

BECK. It isn't from where we were then?

(Pause)

THORPE. I've read about a new weapon it was thought they had.

BECK. The Yanks?

THORPE. Yes.

BECK. The Yanks.

THORPE. It dwarfed the Atom bomb. Dwarfed it, in ten years.

(They stare at the sight)

DOOLAN. Why isn't there any noise?

THORPE. It's a long way off. The pressure waves haven't
reached us yet.

(A thin high sound is heard, like a wail: the boat trembles
finely. There are two reports like muffled rifle shots.
They stare at the sight)

Look at it hard, look at it. That's something to tell your
grandchildren. A page of history turning. Look at it,
turning. We can never go back on that.

(A strong breeze reaches the boat abruptly: the noise sinks
in pitch from a high wail until it becomes the deep, continuous
rumble of the fireball.

Crewroom. The LITTLE GIRL stirs slightly, delicately.

Deck. The boat rocks uneasily, uneasily. They stand
staring at the sight. Fade)

_____

(Fade up. Deck. Close shot of AJUS rubbing his eyes,
which are irritating him: in the background, THORPE and
DOOLAN look up at the sky which is dark and heavy. AJUS
rubs his eyes harder, and blinks to clear them.

147

Galley. ANNA and RAPS cooking. They work quietly, not speaking. ANNA takes a cup of water and crosses out. It is much darker now.

Corridor. She passes engineroom door.

Engineroom. BECK and WILLY at work on the engine, covered in grease. They work fast, not speaking.

Crewroom. The GIRL is now conscious, drinking from the cup. TURK watches)

  *(Deck)

DOOLAN. Like a sort of high fog forming up there.

THORPE. Mm.

DOOLAN. Peculiar, innit?

  (Pause)

THORPE. No sign of that plane.

DOOLAN. No birds, either. There's usually birds around a boat.

  (Pause. AJUS blinks and rubs his eyes again)

DOOLAN. Still.

THORPE. Not up there.

  (They look up at the thick clouds moving fast. It is getting darker)

  *(Galley. A pressure lamp being lit, pumped, and hung up)

RAPS. Better.

  (ANNA serves some rice and takes it out. RAPS stares at some fine white ash on the bottom of the portglass on the exterior)

  *(Crewroom)

ANNA. Here.

  (GRAN takes the dish to feed the GIRL. ANNA feels her

148

forehead)

TURK. What about me, don't I get any?

(He is getting markedly weaker./ ANNA tucks the blanket round the GIRL: suddenly the GIRL takes the spoon and starts to feed herself)

*(Deck)

THORPE. Rain.

DOOLAN. Ayeh.

(It is starting to spatter down lightly)

THORPE. We'll get you in if it gets -

DOOLAN. I'm alright. Anyway there's him. (indicating the wheelhouse)

THORPE. (to AJUS) What's up with your eyes?

AJUS. Hurt.

THORPE. (examining) Was it the flash? - you were looking at the flash all through, weren't you?

AJUS. (suddenly squeals and jerks away)

DOOLAN. Eh?

THORPE. That didn't hurt, did it? Just a bit of rain? -

AJUS. (rubs eyes ferociously)

THORPE. - just rain that's all.

DOOLAN. Don't do that, you'll make it worse.

THORPE. Look at this stuff.

DOOLAN. Eh?

THORPE. In the rain, look. There's stuff like ash.

(He picks some up between finger and thumb. They look at it. /Close up: it is wet and gritty, and looks like wood

ash: it crackles and breaks under pressure./ DOOLAN
shakes a bit off the back of his hand with a sharp jerk.
Without thinking what he is doing he rubs an eye which is
starting to irritate him)

  *(Crewroom)

GRAN. (points to window and exclaims)

TURK. Eh? - look at it.

ANNA. Sleet!

TURK. No.

ANNA. It's sleeting - just a bit.

TURK. Can't be sleet, it's not cold enough. It's warm, even.

   (GRAN talks excitedly to the GIRL, and holds her up to see.
   The GIRL smiles and points at the sight delightedly.)

  *(Galley. RAPS opens the glass and takes a bit of the ash on
   his finger to taste it. Shakes it off sharply. The sensation
   remains. He attempts to rub, then wash, it off: it
   continues to burn. He gets a bit scared)

BECK. (off) Rappers!

RAPS. Yes?

BECK. (off) Let's have your lamp.

  *(Deck. Tiny bits of the sandy ash are swirling down with
   the rain. THORPE wipes bits from his face)

DOOLAN. I think, er...

THORPE. Yes.

DOOLAN. I'll go first and cover you with Beck's firearm.

THORPE. Are you sure that -

DOOLAN. I'm alright. (he peers at wheelhouse) Not there.
   Right.

   (He runs across and gets to companion hatch. Waves to

THORPE. DOOLAN rubs his eyes which are growing
more irritating.)

*(Crewroom. The radio equipment is crackling steadily.
ANNA looks at it. GRAN holds the girl, motionless. TURK
lies on his back, sweating, fevered. No-one moves)

BECK. (off) Lamp! Rappers!

*(Corridor. AJUS comes down the companion ladder, to
join THORPE and DOOLAN at the bottom)

DOOLAN. Right.

THORPE. Did you see him?

AJUS. (shakes head)

DOOLAN. Look, it's getting in here, on the floor.

(They look down. A layer of ash under the hatch area.
THORPE shuts the hatch and bolts it. They stand
undecided)

GIRL. (off: asks a question in Malay, a rising inflection?)

(RAPS crosses the corridor with the lamp, taking it to the
engineroom. THORPE and DOOLAN are suddenly illuminated,
then plunged into darkness)

(Fade up. Interior of the hold of the boat. The walls of the
hold are ribbed with massive rusty girders at two foot
spacings, starting from the heavy keelridge and curving
up the outer walls to top deck level, like the upsidedown
skeleton of a whale. On the exterior of these ribs are
riveted the steel plates that form the outer skin of the boat.
Rusty piping and old wiring runs across the roof and the
walls. /It is here in the hold that the gimcrack construction
of the boat is plainest. Nothing fits or looks in place: all
the materials have been re-used from older boats of all
types and sizes. There are extensive remains of faded white
lettering all over the steel plates of the hull - now jumbled
and meaningless as the plates have been re-used and refitted
time and time again, sometimes upside down, and mostly
quite out of context. Some lettering overlays older, more
faded inscriptions: some have Russian characters, some

could even be badly executed Arabic. It runs over all the
walls and across the roof and floor./ The centre of the
hold goes up to deck level, where there is a large closed
loading-trap. Each end is much lower, to provide room
for the living quarters (fore) and engineroom (aft) on 1st
deck level. A catwalk runs across between the two. / The
walls run with condensation which collects in a pool at the
bottom. Light comes from several small glasses high up
in the outer wall, and one set like a tiny manhole cover in
the deck above their heads. Through them can be caught
glimpses of the 'sleet' falling./ The hold is small and
empty, apart from odd sticks of timber and a few bits of
cable and canvas tied in a bundle.
Looking up steel ladder fixed to the wall of the hold: the
hatch at the top opens and AJUS descends rapidly, followed
by DOOLAN; then TURK being let down on ropes)

TURK. (weak) Down a bit, slowly, and a lovely spot we have
here. Oh yes, just the place for a picnic.

DOOLAN. Easy now, slow.......

TURK. I lost my virginity in a place like this -

DOOLAN. Did you now.

TURK. - very romantic it was, very lovely, I've never been the
same since.

DOOLAN. I can imagine that, yes. Hold him there.

BECK. (above) OK?

TURK. It's quite a place, isn't it? What's all that writing round
the walls?

DOOLAN. What? Oh that. Let's have you Beck.

TURK. Adverts, is it? - or hours of opening? -

(BECK descends)

- oh, an echo! Lal la la la la (deep voice) Your weight
is f -

DOOLAN. Give over now, I thought you were ill.

ANNA. Never felt better.

152

DOOLAN. Well act bloody ill, it's less wearing. (to BECK) Round there. Gently. Up.

(They carry him)

(to TURK) Up and down like a bloody yo-yo.

(In the background, GRAN and ANNA are carrying the GIRL down the ladder)

ANNA. Gently, gently...

AJUS. (Malay: is she better now?)

GRAN. (Malay: she seems to be, oh yes)

ANNA. Mind her shoulder on there now... mind...

TURK. (being carried) It must have been a bit like this for Noah.

DOOLAN. Steady...

TURK. The Ark and all them animals and that, I feel a bit like him down here.

DOOLAN. Two by two.

BECK. Lost his virginity on a boat, did he?

TURK. No - you know, primitive.

RAPS. (descending) Yea.

TURK. Int that right Rappers?

RAPS. One of them old boats, like in the olden days. It's in the Bible.

BECK. Yea?

RAPS. Book of Noah, there's whales and that there. And the man that got swallowed by one and lived inside it for years.

BECK. What, inside a whale?

TURK. That's it, I remember reading about it in the papers.

153

RAPS. No, in the Bible this was, in Ancient Times. Jonah, that was his name, Jonah, in the belly of the whale.

DOOLAN. How did he - you know -

BECK. What.

DOOLAN. How did - they reckon he survived?

TURK. Oh, he had a right time there, had the telly and a little Calor gas cooker - he was that snug the Lord couldn't get him out. Home from home in there, like this place - Oh... ah!...

(They place him on some wooden platform pieces that AJUS has found at one end and laid over the lowest part of the ribbing, covering the pool of rusty water that swills there as the boat sways)

DOOLAN. Aw shut it can't you?

TURK. You have to laugh though, don't you? - you know -

(The GIRL chatters with delight at the sight of the hold, waving her arms at it in her excitement)

ANNA. Careful...

RAPS. Come and join us little love -

(She smiles at him)

- it's all happening down here.

*(Corridor. THORPE passes WILLY water containers, one by one: he hands them down through the hatch./ They work fast, silently, their faces set. Outside, the fallout drifts down)

*(Hold)

BECK. Look at it! -

DOOLAN. Yea?

BECK. - this place. How long we got to stay down here?

DOOLAN. You needn't.

154

BECK. There's not even a toilet.

(The GIRL picks her way over the iron ribs to the platform)

ANNA. (concerned) Careful!

DOOLAN. The greatest distance between us and that stuff, that's what he said.

BECK. But it's stupid, isn't it? - he don't <u>know</u> what it is - just guessing, he said.

DOOLAN. Go back up then.

BECK. <u>I'm</u> not going back up.

(The GIRL jumps the last bit, onto the platform)

```
(RAPS.  That's it!.  )
(                    )
(GRAN.  (Malay)      )  simultaneously
(                    )
(AJUS.  (Malay) !    )
```

ANNA. Come on now, put this round you - right round -

(AJUS squats in a corner, rubbing his eyes)

RAPS. How're you keeping, Turk?

TURK. (suddenly bathed in sweat and weak again) Oh - you know -

RAPS. Good, that's good, soon have you right.

TURK. You going to operate then?

RAPS. You're chirpy, aren't you?

TURK. Wouldn't you be?

RAPS. I am, mate. Time and a half we get for this.

TURK. You what?

RAPS. Maritime service. There's a clause. Time and a half.
(He produces contract)

(DOOLAN, away from the others, bites his thumb, letting his fear emerge a little. /The GIRL stares out of the portglass, watching the slow and gentle fall.

Crewroom. Close shot of portglass, THORPE closing shutter over it. He closes another one, and stands holding it, uncertainly.

Corridor. WILLY lowers the old first-aid box down through the hatch: he descends, carrying the pressure lamp: /THORPE takes a last look round, then follows, closing the hatch behind him, and bolting it.

*Hold. Silence as they descend)

THORPE. (quiet) Right. We'll make a list of what we've got.

WILLY. Food over here, blankets and clothing here, anything else there.

ANNA. Is that the medicine box?

WILLY. Yes.

(She crosses to, and opens it)

THORPE. Pencil? (WILLY shakes head) Er - anyone got, er, anything to write on? Paper or -

ANNA. (paper from box) Here.

BECK. What's he want a list for?

DOOLAN. (shrugs)

BECK. Stupid.

WILLY. Tins of rice, five, six, seven...twelve.

(The list continues)

AJUS. (to TURK) Is he well?

TURK. (indicates "I don't know")

RAPS. (to the GIRL) I bet she never seen anything like that before - no snow or anything. (to AJUS) She wouldn't have seen snow, would she?

156

AJUS. No.

RAPS. Oh, it's lovely. Very cold though - cold. (he shivers dramatically) But lovely, oh beautiful (he adopts beatific expression) We could make a snowman if we was up there - play snowballs. You know what snowballs is? - well -

WILLY. Eight knives, three, four teaspoons, one...er... (he holds up strange Eastern cutlery)

RAPS. - you get the snow like this between your hands, and turn it into a ball, see, by pressing it together like so - see the snow's there, and -

(We see TURK listening, starting to have trouble with his breathing: BECK sits slumped, oblivious: DOOLAN stares out at the fallout slowly drifting down)

- so you get a thing you can throw at people, so you throw it (demonstrates) - and it hits, and - boom! Whoosh! - Splodch! - (great drama: the GIRL giggles) - right down the back of your neck!

TURK. Eh Rappers, you'd have made a lovely Dad!

AJUS. Elah, look!

DOOLAN. What at?

AJUS. (shows GRAN and chatters in Malay: she laughs and whoops)

TURK. What's he got?

RAPS. Something out of the box.

TURK. Box?

AJUS. Look, see, these ladies.

DOOLAN. What box is that then? -

TURK . These what?

DOOLAN. - eh?

157

RAPS. Hey they're pinups - oriental bints, you know - women, sort of.

TURK. Never.

RAPS. Look at them, ent they peculiar. Look, there's dozens of them.

TURK. By God, they'd have to pay me, this lot. (to AJUS) Ugly, int they? - or do you go in for this sort of thing?

AJUS. Oh yes, hahaha.

TURK. Ha ha, look at him! - you must be depraved, darling. They could be my Gran.

RAPS. And here's one of them blokes, look -

(He has found some ordinary snapshots among the pinups. They are unconsciously growing into a single group)

DOOLAN. Oh yea.

RAPS. No, it's a - eh! -

DOOLAN. What.

RAPS. It's him, intit? - him upstairs?

BECK. Show us.

RAPS. - him up there, you know, the captain or whatever he is.

(BECK. There's other stuff look, here - letters and that -)
(   )
(RAPS. Yea?   )
(   )
(BECK. - and a Bible or holy book or something. Silk   )
(scarf... (he pulls stuff roughly out)   )
(   )   overlapping
(RAPS. Look at him, all them medals.   )
(   )
(DOOLAN. Sort of passing out parade.   )
(   )
(TURK. Peculiar-looking, int he?   )
(   )
(RAPS. Sort of like a monkey.   )
(   )

TURK. All that hair on him -

BECK. By God he must have clanked when he - you know -

```
(RAPS.  Come to attention, eh?      )
(                                    )
(DOOLAN.  Ayeh!                      ) simultaneously
(                                    )
(TURK.  - turned corners!            )
```

    (We see the photo. A highly impressive and dignified officer, in splendid Edwardian uniform. They laugh and jeer)

    (Suddenly, over their heads on the deck above, are heard faint and unsteady footsteps. A voice can just be heard, THE CAPTAIN saying something, talking to himself, muttering./ The footsteps stop. Silence)

DOOLAN. (quietly) Eyoop.

GIRL. (Malay to GRAN) ?

GRAN. (tells her to be quiet)

GIRL. (more demanding)

DOOLAN. Nothing we can do for him.

AJUS. (Malay to GIRL, telling her to keep quiet)

GIRL. (chatters)

AJUS. She says will the funny man tell her more about throwing.

    (Pause)

TURK. That's you Rappers.

RAPS. Eh?

TURK. You -

AJUS. Please, can you tell her some more?

RAPS. Er - mm.

    (Pause)

DOOLAN. What will, er....

BECK. Yea.

DOOLAN. What will happen? - to him?

ANNA. Is it going to -

TURK. Let him then.

ANNA. What?

TURK. Let him.

(Pause)

THORPE. Well - (clears throat) - I can only repeat what I said
before -

BECK. Pa!

THORPE. - I don't know for certain. This, erm, falling-out
matter could be active. Atomically. But that may not be so.
I'm not a scientist, I'm not - you can't -

ANNA. But it's from the bomb, isn't it?

THORPE. Bomb?

ANNA. Isn't it?

THORPE. It may have come from the - erm, explosion, we don't
know for cert -

DOOLAN. So what will happen to him?

(Pause)

THORPE. If it -

DOOLAN. Yes, if it's what you think it could be, what will
happen to him?

THORPE. He, erm, may not survive.

DOOLAN. He'll die.

THORPE. Well, that's -

DOOLAN. He'll die.

(Pause)

THORPE. It could happen.

(The footsteps are heard again, faintly, unsteadily, over their heads)

(abruptly disturbed and appealing to them) Believe me, the worst thing is not knowing! I'm only half remembering things I've heard or read. But I don't know, I don't know!

(They listen to the footsteps: they stop. The voice is heard again, mumbling, thick, indistinct. Silence./ AJUS clucks his tongue several times. The GIRL who has been trying to work out what is going on, asks her GRAN in a puzzled whisper: GRAN soothes and shushes her but does not reply./ WILLY produces a book and quietly concentrates on it. / RAPS whistles sadly under his breath./ BECK crosses away and starts to fiddle with oddments on the platform./ THORPE stares into space./ GRAN asks AJUS in Malay what was said. He replies: she sits thinking, her eyes turning to the CHILD)

ANNA. Here. (crosses to GIRL) Look what I've found.

GRAN. (Malay: Oh look what she's got for you!)

GIRL. (Malay: What?)

ANNA. There.

(It is a small, crudely painted child's top)

GIRL. (Malay: What is it, what's it for?)

GRAN. (Malay: It's a top, she'll show you)

ANNA. Look, it goes round, like this - watch -

(She pumps it: it spins and hums)

There, see! -

GIRL. (cries with delight! Malay: Let me see, let me try!)

GRAN. (Malay: You do it then)

DOOLAN. Where did that come from?

ANNA. In the chest there.

RAPS. What would he want with a top?

(GIRL. (Malay: Look, look what I've got!   )
(   )
(AJUS. (Malay: Yes, isn't it good!)   )
(   )
(GIRL. (Malay: It's a top, a spinning top - look, she gave) overlapping
(it me!)   )
(   )
(DOOLAN. It's a rotten little top, but look, all them   )
(colours -   )
(   )
(RAPS. Someone's painted it up. Bright, intit?   )

THORPE. (dully, to himself) Top.

WILLY. Maybe he's got grandchildren.

RAPS. What?

WILLY. That's what he's got it for, and painted it up.

RAPS. (beat) Heck, you make him sound quite human.

(Pause. The top hums. Footsteps above.

TURK and ANNA, close, away from the others)

TURK. Reckon it's over by now?

ANNA. What?

TURK. Back there.

ANNA. On the -

TURK. - the mainland, yes, reckon it's over?

ANNA. Could be.

TURK. It's got to happen though, hasn't it? If it wasn't us,
it'd be someone else. Law of Nature and all that. (he
searches her face for agreement) People have got to -
y'know...

ANNA. What?

TURK. - breathe. Someone's got to do it. Eh? (he searches her face for comment)

(DOOLAN rises and stares out of a glass at the whiteness drifting down)

WILLY. (quietly to THORPE) You alright?

THORPE. Just a bit, erm, feeling a bit sick that's all. And my skin...

WILLY. Skin?

THORPE. - hurts like mad.

WILLY. Itches?

THORPE. Hurts, a pain.

WILLY. All over?

THORPE. No, just - (he indicates exposed skin)

WILLY. Can I -

THORPE. Thanks, I'll be alright. (looks at him) Thanks.

(WILLY looks across at AJUS. He lies curled up in a blanket, eyes open, shivering and sweating./ GRAN starts telling a story in Malay to the GIRL, who sits by her side playing idly with her top as she listens. The OLD WOMAN has lost a lot of her bite: she seems older and weaker./ RAPS approaches BECK and ANNA, who are near TURK)

RAPS. (holds out snapshot)

ANNA. Mm?

RAPS. Guess.

BECK. (takes it) That's you, intit.

ANNA. Who's the woman, then?

RAPS. Can't you, er -

BECK. It's your Mum.

RAPS. It what? (takes it back and peers at it) - my Mum?!

163

ANNA. Who is it then?

RAPS. Teeny, that's my Teeny, we're going to get married.

(They look at him with new interest)

BECK. Teeny.

RAPS. That's not my Mum, my Mum doesn't look anything like
that. It's Teeny, that is.

ANNA. Who's Teeny?

RAPS. When I get back from this lot we're getting married
and having some kids.

BECK. Bit older than you, isn't she?

RAPS. (highly defensive) No, she's not, of course she's not.
Well... a little maybe. I'm not too sure exactly how old
she is. She's been married before, once, but I don't
think that matters does it? - not if you love each other.

BECK. Looks a bit beat up to me.

RAPS. She what? -

ANNA. What happened to...

BECK. Yea.

ANNA. - the, er, first husband.

RAPS. Oh, he went off with another lady, last Michaelmas.
(dutifully) Swine. They didn't have no kids though, so
that's alright.

ANNA. Nice is she?

RAPS. Oh yea - (slightly uncertain) - she's lovely. It's going
to be expensive, but we'll have enough when I get back. Oh
yea. How many kids make a good family do you think? Four?
Five?

TURK. I'd have liked kids. I'd have ... done something then,
you know. Made something after all the... (he leaves it
unfinished) Yea, well.

ANNA. (conditioned reflex) Anyone who brings kids into the world as it is now, must be criminally insane.

TURK. You going to stop them?

(The GIRL sings to herself dreamily as she listens to her GRAN)

But they got to have a chance. Not just... things. They're - y'know, miracles aren't they - jesus, listen to me talking like a tit.

ANNA. No you're not.

TURK. And you can be blind mad to do something about it, and you attack and attack, banging your head against the... and where do you get? - you got to do it, and all it does is - well, you saw those little kids, at -

ANNA. At the -

TURK. - at the school, yes. Poor little -

ANNA. Don't - talk about it.

TURK. Well, that's it, intit? - that's what you achieve. Nothing. Nothing, except that.

(Footsteps overhead. The OLD WOMAN's voice drones on to the CHILD)

And it could all be so marvellous, couldn't it? - all be so... terrific. I mean, it's in people, it's there all right, but how do you... without... How's it done?

(Pause)

Look at it, look at the stuff. It's smaller now, the flakes, you know, like a sort of dust.

(Pause)

ANNA. So - what now?

TURK. Good question. G-o-o-o-d question.

ANNA. People aren't going to...

TURK. What?

165

ANNA. - change, are they? Not just like that. Before the biggest bang of all?

(Outside the white drifts slowly down.

BECK at the far end of the hold, clears his throat)

BECK. Er - got a pencil? Anyone got a pencil please?

DOOLAN. Eh?

BECK. (gestures)

THORPE. Here.

(BECK takes it, and crosses away to far end again, where he has made an arrangement of tarpaulin)

DOOLAN. What you doing, Beck?

(No reply: they watch him)

RAPS. Solid old stuff this, intit? - worth something I'd say.

DOOLAN. Yes?

RAPS. There's a yard round our way would give you a good bit for this. What's that on it, written round the walls?

WILLY. (shakes head)

RAPS. Peculiar, intit?

WILLY. It's just a jumble. (points) That's Russian, isn't it?

RAPS. (tries to pronounce some of it) "Grumbrutt...umt... CROS...STT...wine?..." (shakes his head)

(Pause)

DOOLAN. (to AJUS) Know anything about this round the walls, do you?

AJUS. Know?

DOOLAN. That, look, that writing. Or this boat, know anything about it?

AJUS. (blank)

(WILLY looks at BECK, who is laboriously writing on piece
of card, tongue protruding./Footsteps overhead. They look
up./THORPE crouches, arms clasped round his middle.
His eyes irritate, he feels sick in the stomach and chest./
WILLY notices this. He looks at AJUS./AJUS crouches
motionless)

DOOLAN. Look at it, this thing we're in. None of it fits, does
it? - look at that, that must be from a much bigger boat, and
this, look, that's - oh, that must be a hundred years old.
All built up out of old bits. All that rusty old iron, look at
it. Like when they took down the old watertank in our house.
Or like jankers, do they have jankers on a boat?

TURK. Irons, they put you in irons, don't they?

WILLY. Not any more.

TURK. No?

WILLY. - they call it irons, but it's like a little cell.

(Pause)

TURK. What do you know about it?

WILLY. I was in the Merchant Navy.

RAPS. Yea?

WILLY. Wartime, during the war this was. I did four months
solitary.

TURK. Four months?

WILLY. I had these Holy Pictures pinned up inside my locker,
it was them.

(Pause)

RAPS. Holy Pictures?

WILLY . The other blokes had pin-ups, you know, girls, on the
inside of their locker doors. Well I had Holy Pictures.

(They stare at him. WILLY talks quietly, with great
simplicity)

There was an inspection one day and when the PO saw my

pictures, he - well, he didn't like them. Told me to take
them down, thought it was some sort of a joke I think.
Anyhow, I asked him why shouldn't I have them if the
others had their pin-ups. So he tore them down. So I put up
another lot and next inspection they marched me off. I got
a week then: the next time it was a month, then four months.

(Pause)

RAPS. What were the pictures of?

WILLY. Oh, the Infant Jesus, that sort of thing.

DOOLAN. Four months solitary?

WILLY. Yes.

DOOLAN. How did you...?

WILLY. I think I started to go a bit mad near the end. Anyhow,
the MO got me out.

RAPS. What happened?

WILLY. Mm?

RAPS. - when you were released.

WILLY. Oh - (thin smile) - I put them up again.

(Silence)

(At the far end of the hold, BECK clears his throat noisily.
They look up)

BECK. "Engaged".

(He holds a piece of card on which is written a crude "E":
he turns it over to show a "V")

"Vacant"

(They look blankly at him: he demonstrates)

"Engaged" (turns it over) "Vacant". It's a toilet.

(He indicates a grim looking structure of tarpaulin he has
made right in the forecorner of the boat, and rests the card
against it. They stare blankly. He demonstrates again)

168

"Engaged" (turns it over) "Vacant" See?

(He stands there glowing with pleasure)

Good innit? It's a toilet! (he looks round hopefully) Er - anyone...?

(They stare at him transfixed./ Footsteps above their heads, irregular, dragging across the deck. Fade)

(Fade up. Hold. The air is thick and close. A heavy thud shudders through the boat, jerking over tins and small objects)

(THORPE. What is it?   )
(   )
(BECK. What's he doing?   ) simultaneously
(   )
(RAPS. We hit something.   )

    (Pause)

BECK. Stopped.

DOOLAN. No, he's -

RAPS. Yea.

DOOLAN. Bit of a -

BECK. - I hear him.

    (Pause)

TURK. (very weak) We hit something, it wasn't him upstairs.

BECK. No? He's still around.

THORPE. Now now.

BECK. He's -

THORPE. - it's too... he wouldn't still be around now. Not now.

    (Pause. This sinks in slowly)

RAPS. What - was it then?

DOOLAN. Rock or -

BECK. We hit something.

DOOLAN. Yea.

RAPS. - drifted against it.

> (Close shot of TURK. He looks straight up at the tiny
> windowglass right above him, set in the deck, and watches
> the slow drift down onto it)

THORPE. I think we should... move away from the sides. It's
probably accumulated on the deck and the further away we
are...

DOOLAN. Right then.

> (They start moving in towards the centre, gathering on the
> platform)

THORPE. I imagine it's all collecting on deck, and the
radiation maybe... anyhow, if we're away from the walls...

> (They move slowly, cumbersomely, the sick being helped by
> the others)

RAPS. Getting hot.

AJUS. No-where for air to...

BECK. No.

> (The GIRL covers her GRANDMOTHER over with a blanket:
> she smiles up at her./ They finish moving onto the platform,
> now a tiny, compact group. They sit there for a while not
> speaking; just sit, as if waiting./ Then TURK speaks very
> quietly, taking up the thought now in all their minds, death).

TURK. (barely audible) There was this mad old woman, I was a
boy; the Gull woman, that's what we all called her.

ANNA. The what?

TURK. Used to live off gulls' eggs and muck; mad as a hatter,
lived miles out on the Marsh where I come from, in a little

170

kennel thing. You don't have gulls in Australia, it's too sunny.

ANNA. Yes, we have gulls.

TURK. Terrible bogey woman she was. I was very ill once and all through I thought she was standing over my bed, this old woman. But my little brother talked to her once, and he said she was alright, really.

ANNA. Got a brother have you?

TURK. No no. (silence) He gave me this. (he pulls out the tiny fossil fernleaf, on a chain around his neck) Good, innit?

ANNA. It's a fossil.

TURK. Fernleaf, it's a little fernleaf, see? Lovely, isn't it?

BECK. Did he die then?

TURK. (stares at the fossil)

RAPS. He's bad, isn't he? Is he - will he be OK?

(It is getting hot and close as the air thickens, making a steamy, slightly drunken atmosphere: people move unsteadily)

WILLY. (with chart)... only name is this Marfa, or - Tematangi.

DOOLAN. Ayeh.

WILLY. We could be near that.

THORPE. You know of it?

DOOLAN. Tematangi?

BECK. Battle, wasn't it?

DOOLAN. Slaughter, more like, bloody massacre.

AJUS. Is very dangerous, much wreckage, very shallow.

DOOLAN. Don't you remember? About '43. A huge American landing expedition just all shot up. There was, oh, tens of thousands of them packed like sardines into these open landing craft: there was some sort of mistake, I can't remember what - anyhow, day come and the Jap planes found them and just mowed them down.

AJUS. Was terrible, took many hours to kill them all. They jumping in the water, screaming - but they just - (he imitates a plane machine-gunning) -

DOOLAN. Ayeh.

AJUS. Is very shallow here, you see into the water, and oh, like glass, many many miles of old rifles and helmets and clothes and the boats on the bottom of the sea full of gunholes, and oh thick, thick with these men, moving...

DOOLAN. Moving?

AJUS. Under the water, the water move them...

BECK. All their old clothes I expect, nothing in them but bones now.

WILLY. You've seen it?

AJUS. No no, but my brother - No boats will come here. Frightened.

BECK. Frightened?

DOOLAN. Easy to get holed with all the wreckage around.

(Pause)

WILLY. Was that what we thumped into, do you reckon, and scraped along?

RAPS. Could be, couldn't it?

DOOLAN. Bloody terrible.

WILLY. Useless.

DOOLAN. Eh?

WILLY. If you get killed <u>doing</u> something, then...

ANNA. Yes.

WILLY. But when it's just...

172

DOOLAN. ...like cattle...

(There is a dull scraping sound as the boat sheers gently
past a submerged wreck. / They are breathing deeply: the air
is thick and they are starting to feel drunk. Their speaking
is slurred and hesitant)

AJUS. Is said - if you come here, the soldiers push your boat
away.

RAPS. They do what?

AJUS. Yes, is true. They say "We can do nothing now,
except say go, go from this fighting" - and push your boat
with their hands, and it move away, like - by itself.

(Pause)

DOOLAN. Touch of the old horrors.

THORPE. No, you can understand it.

DOOLAN. Can you?

THORPE. That's what I'd try and do. If I died like that -
fighting a war, a just war, but - pointlessly. I'd shout out! -
(but he says it very quietly) - "Did our deaths make any
difference, did they mean anything? Is the world a better
place to live in? Oh, make it worthwhile that we died".

DOOLAN. And would anyone hear?

(Silence. The frame of the boat creaks and sighs)

*(We see the fallout descending on the sea. A great desert of
whiteness)

*(Hold. The air is much thicker. They are lying inert, having
difficulty with breathing. Their faces glow with sweat)

ANNA. Can I get you anything?

TURK. No thanks.

BECK. Perhaps we should keep watch.

TURK. Oh yea?

BECK. In turns, y'know.

RAPS. (photo)

DOOLAN. (takes it)

RAPS. My woman.

DOOLAN. Ah.

RAPS. Are you - were you ever married?

    (Pause)

DOOLAN. You'll make a good dad.

RAPS. Yea?

DOOLAN. Oh aye, you will. You'll be good with kids.

RAPS. Well they're lovely, aren't they, lovely things. Give
you a...give you a reason.

    (Pause)

DOOLAN. Yes, well it's taken me all of my life to stay out of
that sort of thing.

RAPS. Stay out of it?

DOOLAN. Yes. Don't fancy it.

RAPS. No?

DOOLAN. This did me, this life. No bother, and - it's clean.
I like that. You know where you are. (pause) Got a date fixed,
have you?

RAPS. When I get back.

DOOLAN. Ah. (looks at him)

RAPS. I'll have got enough money then, you see - from this job,
we can marry on that.

    (Pause)

DOOLAN. Fine, good.

RAPS. If she's... you know, if nothing's...

DOOLAN. Yes.

RAPS. - while I've been away.

(There is a long scraping sound as they drift and sheer past wreckage./ANNA sits motionless, breathing deeply and with difficulty. Her shirt is undone and a piece of string round her neck underneath has fallen out)

TURK. What's that?

ANNA. Mm?

TURK. There.

ANNA. - oh -

(It is a wedding ring. She hides it)

TURK. What happened?

ANNA. Mm?

TURK. To - er - (he nods to the ring) Needed kids, did he?

(ANNA turns away)

BECK. (bares his stomach) See that?

TURK. (looks at it)

BECK. That scar, look.

TURK. Yea?

BECK. Appendix, 1946. And this here see? - stomach blockage 1949. Big op, that was, specialist's job.

TURK. Lovely.

BECK. They took photos. So - (close to TURK) - it'll be alright, see?

(Pause)

THORPE. I should have stayed - at home - by the fire.

(Pause)

RAPS. I dunnarf feel ill.

(Pause. Slowly the GIRL relinquishes her hold on her
GRANDMOTHER who has sunk from sleep to unconscious-
ness, and crossed to ANNA. / DOOLAN lies back, trying to
mouth the words on the wall, silently.

Mix to: the fallout drifting down over the sea.

Mix to: hold. It is dark now. Pan around the faces, muzzy,
just out of focus, heaving for air)

WILLY. Getting heavier again.

BECK. Yea?

WILLY. Out there.

(He indicates the portglass set in the deck over their heads
like a tiny glass manhole cover. The fallout is building up
on it like a snowdrift./ Pan past THORPE, eyes closed,
huddled)

GIRL. (Malay, quietly)

AJUS. Water?

ANNA. (whisper) Sorry, it's not safe.

(Pause)

RAPS. I wish I could shave.

(There is a long scraping sound as the boat scores past a
wreck)

DOOLAN. One of my socks is on inside out.

(Pause)

RAPS. Beck.

BECK. Mm?

RAPS. Have you ever seen anyone... you know... dead?

BECK. (turns and looks at him)

176

RAPS. I haven't. (pause) My first job, this

BECK. (turns away)

RAPS. What does it... what does it look like?

BECK. (after a long pause) Nothing.

RAPS. Eh?

BECK. Nothing.

(DOOLAN is crying silently. The GIRL lies curled in ANNA's lap, eyes open.

There comes the sound of whispering of countless voices: it starts from silence, grows to a faint but audible level, then builds in volume until it seems to fill the vessel with sound./We see each in turn listening, their faces blurred, heaving for breath, not sure if the sound is real or in their own imaginations./ It builds in volume to a crescendo of whispering voices, each striving frantically, desperately, to make itself heard above the rest, fighting to get its message through to us, tens of thousands of men. There are little scurrying and scratching noises against the hull as if trying to force their way in./ A thud from the boat as it again hits the submerged wreck: instant and total silence./ A slow, irregular slithering movement is heard on deck, as if something were dragging itself along./ In the small manhole port-glass above them, appears the CAPTAIN's face, pressed against it, distorted, staring down at them. Fade)

_____

(Fade up. Hold. Sunlight streams in through the side and top glasses. The group has not moved in the slightest. The boat is completely motionless./Close shot of TURK. He opens his eyes. We see his point of view - the manhole glass directly above him, frosted over with an inch of white, snowlike fallout. The outline of the CAPTAIN's head can be seen, turned on its side and indistinct through the whiteness. No part of his face can be seen./TURK moves his head and looks around him. He sees the hold, with sunshine now striking across the far wall, giving everything a crystal clarity, a sharp edged definiteness./He lies back again and tries to grapple with his thoughts. He rocks his head from side to side, rapidly: then suddenly stops and lies still.

There are movements from the rest of the group./ DOOLAN

177

opens his eyes: then his mind catches up and he wakes: he
realises the crisis has passed: closes them, opens them
again: pause: he starts to tremble. To stop himself he
sits up abruptly on the edge of the platform, feet between
the girders, and holds himself there stiffly. Starts to
tremble again: rocks to and fro, both arms clasped round
his middle. / ANNA wakes, finding the GIRL curled up asleep
in her lap: instinctively protects her, putting her arms
tighter around her: because they are in the centre of the
group she does not at first see the changes, but she feels
the stillness of the boat, and tries to look about her. She
turns to TURK who returns her look. / BECK sits, eyes open,
motionless, like a frog. / RAPS lies still, foetally, his eyes
still closed, breathing quickly as though he has a high
temperature. His clothes are wringing wet. / THORPE and
GRAN lie motionless. / WILLY's attitude is the strangest: it
is almost as if he was expecting this. He sits up sharply
and takes a deep breath, as if refreshed by a night's sleep
and about to tackle the job in hand again. / TURK, with great
effort, gets himself up onto one elbow, and then to a sitting
position. / The GIRL wakes, quite normally and naturally, and
smiles up at ANNA. Cut to black.

Cut up to: corridor, the companion hatch, seen from below.
It is unbolted and swung open. Brilliant sun and blue sky.
The ash lies about half an inch thick, with larger lumps of up
to an inch across. Some falls in, glistening and sparkling like
snow. WILLY turns and re-descends.

Engineroom. He opens the shutter over a wallglass and the
sun streams in. The enging lies cold. He looks about, finds
a smaller, batter-run installation, starts it.

Hold. They hear the warm sound of the small engine.

Deck. The sluices start to run on deck, swilling the ash
away, and out through the scuppers. Pan along motionless
body of the CAPTAIN, up his leg, side, along his arm to his
fingers. Continue pan with lump of ash till it falls over the
side. Cut to black.

Cut up to: Deck. BECK and AJUS stand near wheelhouse. The
sun dazzles. We see their viewpoint: the sun dazzling up
from the swilling fallout.

Deck. ANNA holds the GIRL's hand: they stand motionless.

Corridor. RAPS sits on foot of companion ladder: DOOLAN on the ledge to galley. Motionless. Tick of a wristwatch is heard with crystal clarity.

Hold. Wide shot entire hold, THORPE, GRAN, TURK, all tiny in centre. Close shot of TURK. He is seeing tiny pieces of matter, the roughness of the iron, the sun shining through a single drop of moisture against a girder, the folds in a loose piece of cloth, a minute flying insect, the sun on the tarpaulin of BECK's lavatory. He reaches out a finger and feels the texture of the tiny pieces of rust on the girder, old wood of the platform, the texture of the blanket, dazzling, in his eyes, like the rarest jewels.

Galley. DOOLAN, BECK, RAPS, WILLY, AJUS, crammed into the tiny room, all talking together, eating rice pudding out of tins with the hunger of days.

Hold. ANNA and TURK are exploding into words.

(TURK. We're through then, aren't we, we got through!)
(Listen to them, will you - the racket!   )
(   )
(   ) sim.
(ANNA. I thought - we're stuck in it, like statues, you)
(know - statues you play when you're a child, we're)
(always going to be like this... (laughs shrilly)   )

(An almighty crash above.

Galley. A table has fallen over, RAPS and BECK with it. They lie on the floor, roaring with laughter, the others shouting at them.

(Hold. The LITTLE GIRL, in foreground, talking gently to)
(her unconscious GRAN, as if trying to calm her and make)
(her sleep)   )
(   ) sim.
(TURK. listen to them - (laughs) - who have they got up   )
(there, sounds like a pack of schoolgirls!   )

(Cut to close shot of THORPE as he comes round: racket continues in background)

THORPE. (whisper) Turk. Turk.

TURK. Hallo hallo, yes - Thorpey lad!

THORPE. (incredulous) We got through then?

179

TURK. Speak up me old love.

THORPE. We got through!

TURK. We're still here, yes, don't ask me how.

THORPE. ... not possible!

GIRL. (Malay, to TURK)

ANNA. What's that darling?

GIRL. (repeats it, and indicates "sleep", pointing to her GRAN)

ANNA. Yes, she's asleep.

(A boom echoes throughout the vessel, vibrating and humming
through its taut metal frame: the main engine is starting
just above their heads.

Engineroom. The huge flywheel slowly edging into motion,
the pistons stirring, gradual build-up of power and noise.

Hold. The noise, coming from just over their heads, is
deafening. TURK is trying to struggle up)

(TURK. Here, give us a hand a minute - Come on woman,)
(help can't you -   )
(   ) sim.
(ANNA. Don't be so stupid as to think - you're in much too)
(dangerous a state to -   )

(Another loud hum adds to the build-up, and the frame vibrates
more)

TURK. Listen, isn't that good? Where are we going though?

ANNA. They've - er, had a meeting over that. Careful -

TURK. They've what?

ANNA. In the galley, they had a meeting.

(TURK. I'll - where are they, what are they doing? Why) over-
(wasn't I -   )
(   )
(ANNA. Steady... you mustn't move, don't be so -   )

180

(TURK. Shut it woman, I'm going up top (protests) I'm) overlap
(going up on deck, I can't just...) overlap

(The LITTLE GIRL looks over)

You come too, my love. She'll be alright, your Gran.
Cover her up. Come on, give us your hand. Thorpe?

THORPE. I'll be alright. (whisper) Did they - did they find the
old man?

ANNA. Yes.

THORPE. Was he - how did he look?

ANNA. Lying on his side, all twisted up.

THORPE. Hm. When they put him over - into the water - see
they do it... you know, with a bit of respect.

(He turns his face away to the wall)

Mix to: the propellers coming fully into play, churning white
water./ The boat starts to turn on its axis)

*Deck. ANNA has half carried TURK up the companion ladder.
They emerge on deck into the sunlight with the LITTLE GIRL)

TURK. Oh! Sun!

ANNA. They're heading for Easter Island.

TURK. How far's that?

ANNA. Something like 200 miles.

TURK. Isn't there anything nearer?

ANNA. Yes, but there's fighting all around the smaller islands.
They want to pull right clear of all that and make for where
they know it's OK. It's also where she comes from.

TURK. Eh?

ANNA. Her, you know, the little girl.

TURK. Yea?

ANNA. Where she was born. Ajus was saying. Evacuated after

her parents were killed, to live with her Gran. During the war, you know.

TURK. Aye, the war.

(Gulls cry overhead: TURK looks up)

ANNA. Willy's going back.

TURK. Where to?

ANNA. Back there. Where we were. To the fighting.

RAPS. Well, look, it's laughing boy!

(BECK. Cripes, never expected to see you about again!)
(   )
(DOOLAN. Well well, look who's turned up.   ) sim.
(   )
(WILLY. Hallo Turk, how are you?   )

(The boat heaves in motion: they shout)

*Deck (later). TURK lying out in the sun on deck: ANNA has put a blanket over him. The GIRL is apart from them, singing away to herself)

TURK. Look at them.

ANNA. Who?

TURK. Beck and Rappers.

ANNA. Eh?

TURK. Heads together. Doesn't take long, does it?

(Pause)

DOOLAN. You talk like as if...

TURK. What?

DOOLAN. - people learn.

TURK. Don't they?

DOOLAN. (derisive noises)

(The GIRL sings)

TURK. By God, she's got a pair of lungs, just listen to her!
Who's she singing to?

ANNA. Look - a seagull!

TURK. That's not a gull that's a -

ANNA. That's a seagull, I know a seagull don't I?

TURK. (grins)

DOOLAN. Means we're getting nearer, anyroad.

TURK. So I should bloody hope.

ANNA. How long?

DOOLAN. Oh, a day. Not far now.

(The CAPTAIN's body being gently lowered over the side into
the water: it is seen to move down slowly in the green,
until out of sight./The boat moves forward, full power now./
The LITTLE GIRL, standing high up forward in the sunshine
and looking out ahead, singing and singing at the top of her
voice)

THE LAST ENEMY

CHARACTERS

TURK (now 59)

ANNA (now 48)

CELLY (now 29)

PETTA (9)

GLANVILLE (36)

BRUNO (6)   )
)
CLARE (8)   )
)
PERRY (10)   )
)
VINCENT (12)   )   (the Godfrays' children)
)
CATHY (14)   )
)
CRISPIN (16)   )
)
AGNES (18)   )

THE GULL WOMAN

(Fade up: close shot of a nine-year old MALAWI GIRL, her face shadowed and half-hidden by a tattered blanket over her head. CELLY, ·a Filipino, is hurriedly straightening her rags of clothing, whispering and muttering to her. GLANVILLE sits smoking./ In the background, a loudspeaker address can be heard)

VOICE. (fast and urgent)...just getting them out somehow, while they're still alive - just as they are, with nothing but what they stand up in...just getting them out of the madhouse-and-bloodbath that their homes have become, and over to us here where we can do something. That's why I'm up here now -

(Pulling back: they are behind the speaker's platform, among a mass of cable and equipment. A small monitor screen shows the platform with the speaker and several others on it)

- for you, for you, to say to all these kids - "All right, loves, you're safe now, you're out of all the screaming lunacy that's turned your homes like into a butcher's shop - at least here we've started to come sane, we'll help you, we'll look after you". And I'll tell you something: helping them is the only way we're going to stay sane ourselves, and stop what's happened there from happening here, you know that?

(Cut to the platform: it is the base of Nelson's Column in Trafalgar Square. Behind it hangs an enormous photo of a grossly undernourished child sitting in a ruined house./ It is TURK who is speaking, making an affectation of his rough 'straight-from-the-shoulder' style, and giving it the full dramatic works./ A cold February day in 1976.

TURK. For we're only still here ourselves - alive and kicking - through sheer bloody luck, aren't we my loves? - Eh? - How many times in the last ten years has it looked dead certain we hadn't a hope of lasting out till now, till 1976,

187

without the final Big Bang? - that it had to happen, we
couldn't avoid it, there's so much madness in us - remember?
But, like the drunken man said when he'd crossed Niagara
Falls on a tightrope - 'Here we are somehow, surprise
surprise'.

(Cross-cutting with silent crowd of all ages listening in
Trafalgar Square)

- and not completely maimed or totally mad neither - though
Christ, when you think what human beings have perpetrated
these last sixty years alone, it's a wonder little babies are
still born sane, innit?

But they are. Sane, and clear, and perfect - no credit to us,
ha! There's a miracle for you, good as any in the Bible!
And the nightmare's started passing now, we turned some sort
of corner - and we all felt it, didn't we? -

(We see ANNA, now 48, one of the party on the platform: her
face is thin and pinched, she huddles in her coat from the
cold)

- like someone walked over your grave, like birds in a
flight all changing direction at once. We started to - wake
up somehow, to look round just like some bloody madman
who's been running berserk with an axe smashing up anyone
he comes across, suddenly bashes his head - by accident,
y'know, on something - and sort of starts to come round
somehow and - and he looks at the axe in his hand, and all the
blood...and he says - "What's been happening... what have I
been doing?"... and a shudder goes through him, a change.
And very, very slowly, his sanity starts to... seep back.

(We see newsreel and TV cameras. TURK, seen close to,
looks older than his 59 years, ill and strained, but
absolutely sure of himself)

I say starts. Oh, we've a long, long way to go yet before
the world is a fit place to live in, but we have started. OK
then, how are we going to keep it up? -

(He leans right forward over the rail and speaks low and quiet)

We carry it on ourselves. We just do small in our own
homes what we want done big the world over. Simple? -
that's why I'm here and where this little girl comes in.
Because it's not The Management that's going to decide if
we're going to continue towards some sort of sanity or not,

not some politicians or computers somewhere, but us, right now, you and me.

*(Back of platform)

GLANVILLE. (getting up) This is us.

CELLY. Come on darling.

(TURK's voice continues in background)

GLANVILLE. (stubbing cigarette) How they love him.

CELLY. Well, he's good.

GLANVILLE. Oh, he's a bloody genius.

*(Platform)

TURK. ...and over five hundred of these kids arrived in London an hour ago, and five hundred will be arriving every day now for weeks. They've got nothing, they don't speak English, they've just like walked out of a nightmare.

I want every family to adopt one. There'll be no government allowances, no grants, nothing like that. Every family - not just the people next door or over the road - you, your family. They're the result of our world, these kids - they've known nothing but slaughter and starvation and disease and almost unbelievable misery.

I'm here to welcome the little girl we are going to adopt, my family. Here she is.

*(Back of platform)

GLANVILLE. Right.

(CELLY picks up the CHILD and they mount the steps to the platform.)

*(Platform)

TURK. There we are then. There. That's right.

(The CHILD's free hand is put into TURK's, and he leads her forward to the front of the platform. In spite of the buildup, her appearance is shocking. Her thin body moves jerkily, and she still clutches the blanket over her head, hiding most of her

189

face. The crowd are silent. TURK lifts the GIRL up and stands her on the rostrum in front of him. She stands there motionless, eyes quivering but seeing nothing, seemingly unaware of where she is or what is happening)

What's - what's your name, darling? Eh? Have you got a name?

CELLY. (shakes head)

TURK. Where's she from?

CELLY. Northern Malawi, a copper-town called Zomkibu.

TURK. In the middle of...

CELLY. - of some of the worst fighting, yes. It was a town of fifty thousand people, but it's just rubble now. We found her just... crawling about on it.

(Pause. The CHILD stands stock still)

TURK. Well, can we see you darling, eh? - can we see your face?

(He gently tries to remove the blanket. Immediately she shrieks and clutches it in place. The packed crowd watch silently. The CHILD makes two thin, reedy sounds, like a strange bird)

CHILD. Pet. Ta.

(Silence)

Pet...ta.

(TURK lifts her up onto his hip and holds her there in the face of the world)

Pet-ta.

(A party crammed into the small rooms of 'Campaign', all talking loudly and at once. Champagne./ Round the walls hang posters from various campaigns, each prominently featuring TURK)

GLANVILLE. Marvellous man, marvellous, rang the bell loud

190

and clear -

CELLY. It was very good Turk -

GLANVILLE. - if you'd told them to adopt homosexual Polar
Bears they'd have jumped at it.

TURK. It seemed to go off alright, didn't it?

GLANVILLE. Alright? You could have heard a pin drop at
the end there -

TURK. Yes, yes -

GLANVILLE. (filling TURK's glass) - had them in the palm of
your hand, the palm of your hand, boy, best thing you've
ever done! -

TURK. Whoa! - (laughs)

GLANVILLE. - and that girl, that little slip of a... where did
you get her?

CELLY. I said, Zomkibu!

(GLANVILLE. Oh, she really did come from Zom -   )
(   ) overlapping
(CELLY. Well of course she did!   )
(   )
(GLANVILLE. - couldn't have got anyone better if you'd)
(searched from here to Oxfam!   )

TURK. (moving away) Right then.

GLANVILLE. And the ratings were... (calls after him) Do you
know, more people watched you than Fanny Cradock?

(MAN. (pushing in) Congratulations, absolutely brilliant)
(performance -   ) sim.
(   )
(WOMAN. (kissing him) Oh you were superb, the best   )
(I've ever -   )

GLANVILLE. Am I overdoing it?

CELLY. I'm sure you mean it.

GLANVILLE. Oh, I do, every word! - feeling a bit sorry for

191

the old swine -

CELLY. There's no need.

GLANVILLE. Yes, but his swansong and all that, last time in
the bright lights, last time launching the big appeal (quickly)
Oh, it has to be, it has to be of course, but still...

CELLY. Where's the little girl?

GLANVILLE. Mm? Oh, I heard Anna saying something about
taking her back to the hotel to clean her up a bit.

CELLY. (making to go) Then I think I'll just -

GLANVILLE. She's alright, isn't she? Nothing wrong with her?

CELLY. (look)

GLANVILLE. Well, no worse than any of the others. And there
are plenty of other doctors besides you whom Anna can
call in if -

CELLY. Yes, I suppose so.

GLANVILLE. Well then. You deserve a break, girl, you only
just got back from it all.

CELLY. (nods)

GLANVILLE. Hey! - seen this? -

(He holds up evening paper: on the front is a large and highly
dramatic photo of TURK holding up the CHILD)

Fantastic, isn't it? - God bless him and I love his guts but -
boy! (shakes head) - fantastic!

CELLY. Effective, though.

GLANVILLE. (not so sure) Ooooooh....

CELLY. It gets results.

GLANVILLE. You say that? Compared with an entire department
of the United Nations?

CELLY. It's not a question of -

GLANVILLE. Listen, girl: when you lot at the UN take over
these little organisations next year, just stand back. It may
not be so - (newspaper) - personal, but by God it'll get the
food in the tummies or whatever, and double quick too,
without all the... bleeding hearts. Look - I love your old
Turk, he's done miracles the fifteen years plus he's been
at it, by sheer... pigheadedness, slog, call it anything you
like except professionalism. But there's a revolution
happening, no place for this sort of thing any more!

CELLY. (after thought) You mean - looking after the little girl
himself?

   *(Hotel bathroom. The bath is running, and ANNA is
   undressing the GIRL, throwing rags of clothing over a chair
   one by one. She leaves the piece of blanket till last)

ANNA. Come on now. Come on. Please. Mustn't get it wet.
(she lifts a corner of the blanket and finds the GIRL's hand
underneath, clutching it so tightly that the knuckles show
white./ ANNA hesitates, then picks her up and puts her in
the bath, blanket and all. She sits there in the water,
motionless. ANNA watches)

   *(Committee rooms again)

GLANVILLE. And suppose he does, suppose he does look after
her! - I mean really, himself. That would be village-hall-
amateur, wouldn't it? - wastage of unique manpower on
something that God knows how many schmaltz-starved Mums
of both sexes could do standing on their ears?

CELLY. But that would be -

GLANVILLE. He won't though. He's changed the year you've been
away. Got more than half an eye on the immortality stakes
now. (CELLY incredulous) What? (calls) Turk!

CELLY. No - Glan -

GLANVILLE. You going to have time boy?

TURK. (arriving back) Eh?

GLANVILLE. With everything else? - time to look after her?
(he holds up the evening paper)

TURK. Aye aye, I haven't seen this one.

GLANVILLE. (shouting over the racket) Marvellous man,   193 should win an Oscar or something! -

CELLY. And you are going to have time aren't you? - to look after her?

TURK. Oh I expect somebody else will do most of the actual... er, it's good, isn't it?

GLANVILLE. (eye on CELLY) Good? If we don't hit every jackpot in the shop with this one, I'll adopt all the little baskets myself!

(TURK catches their look)

TURK. (abruptly) Listen, I'm off now.

GLANVILLE. OK son, and -

TURK. But I want to talk to you, OK? - come down to my place.

GLANVILLE. (surprise) What, out in the wilds there?

TURK. (touchy) If it's not too much trouble.

GLANVILLE. Alright, alright...

CELLY. Couldn't he come down with me on Thursday? Is that soon enough?

TURK. Yes, sure, I didn't know you were, er -

CELLY. Thursday, three days time.

GLANVILLE. What's it about then?

TURK. OK, make it then - phone me, OK?

(He goes abruptly, pushing his way through the crowd, who clap him as he leaves)

GLANVILLE. Losing his sense of something. And I thought you were mad at me?

CELLY. Well... maybe I've known you too long. And maybe, coming straight back from it all... I operated on 47 children the day before yesterday.

GLANVILLE. Yes, so you said.

194

CELLY. Did I?

GLANVILLE. You can get too close to it, you know -

CELLY. Mm.

GLANVILLE. - to see clearly, get the best results. You've got
to be that bit removed.

CELLY. You can get too far away too.

GLANVILLE. Yes. (beat) <u>And</u> I have a gracious invitation to
visit the Ivory Tower, how about that then?

(Pause)

CELLY. How about that!

GLANVILLE. That's away from the vulgar herd if you like, I
thought ordinary mortals weren't allowed within wide oceans
of the place - only been asked once before.

CELLY. I remember.

GLANVILLE. (at a TURK poster) Bloody madman. He's
fighting this take-over like mad, expect that's what it's about.

CELLY. He's not well, you know.

GLANVILLE. Ha!

CELLY. - and I think he's a lot worse the year I've been away.
It's years of colossal overwork, -

GLANVILLE. But he's stubborn, stubborn as an old wall.
It's in the interests of the kids, for God's sake! -

CELLY. He's dedicated, Glan; it's not easy for him; think
what he's done in fifteen years!

GLANVILLE. He's dedicated, girl, I've never doubted it.
Question is - (holds up photo in paper) - who to?

*(Hotel bedroom: TURK is sitting up in bed, studying and
annotating papers, lips moving)

ANNA. (entering from second bedroom) She won't sleep.

TURK. (abrupt) Eh?

195

ANNA. The little girl, she won't sleep.

TURK. Later.

ANNA. What?

TURK. Later, she'll sleep later.

ANNA. She's got that blanket thing still.

(Pause)

Go and see her, eh?

TURK. In the morning.

ANNA. You haven't seen her at all.

(Silence. TURK mutters. She gets into bed)

Do you know, they don't know anything about her? Who her parents were, her name, even her age can't be worked out properly because her diet's been so appalling... There were only a few hundred adults survived in that town, so they lined up the kids and tried to have as many identified as possible. No-one recognised her.

TURK. What's that blanket thing she's got?

ANNA. I don't know. But it's...

TURK. Mm?

ANNA. I don't know. (beat) She's ill you know.

TURK. Yes.

ANNA. I don't mean diet.

(Pause)

TURK. What then?

ANNA. Not that sort of illness.

TURK. Eh? (he looks at her) How can you tell? You can't tell. (beat) What sort of illness?

ANNA. Oh...

TURK. She's shocked, of course - she'll have to be treated gently for a few days.

ANNA. (after looking at him with quiet incredulity) Yes, I should think she's shocked.

(TURK abruptly puts papers aside: takes pills from bottle at bedside)

(deep breath) How was the party?

TURK. Oh, you know.

ANNA. Lovely, noise, hooray, people.

TURK. (grunts)

ANNA. - you don't like people, do you? You do lip service to liking them, but -

TURK. Yes, alright, OK, I know.

ANNA. Go and see her, eh?

(Pause. TURK lights a cigarette and draws in deeply)

I phoned up home.

TURK. (silence)

ANNA. Perry's got a cold.

TURK. (staccato) Yes. Yes.

(Silence. ANNA turns off the bedside lamp and lies out. TURK sits smoking)

(to himself) It's so big...

ANNA. What is?

TURK. Mm? Oh - (papers) - all this. The Job, you know.

ANNA. (ironic) Putting the World to Rights?

TURK. The next project, you know, the next campaign. There's so much needs doing in the world, you get sort of drowned by it, overwhelmed by it, just thinking about it.

197

ANNA. You and Jesus Christ, you mean.

(TURK smokes. ANNA turns away on her side and looks
towards the second bedroom./ Pan across with her look,
through the door into the second room: close in on the
GIRL, lying eyes open. The blanket has fallen away, and
for the first time we see her face clearly./ She is almost
bald: her body is thin and boney: and her eyes are enormous
and sunk in dark sockets./ The warm, fresh-smelling sheets
and blankets she lies in look grotesque against her skin.
Fade)

(Fade up. Close shot of CLARE, aged 8, wrapped up
against the cold wind)

CLARE. Here they come! (she turns and shouts) Here they
come!

(She is high up on the flat roof of TURK's house: she waves
to a group of children down on the beach below, who shout
back and start running up towards the house./ Longshot of
the car approaching at some distance along an unmade-up
track, across the flat shingly wastes of Dengemarsh

Inside the car. TURK driving, ANNA with her arm round the
GIRL in the back. Silence./ ANNA looks wearily through
the side window. Her viewpoint: clumps of low dark sloe and
gorse bushes in between great sweeps of bare shingle curving
gently away for mile after mile into the distance. No trees
or grass, no buildings of any sort except TURK's house.
Patches of snow remain here and there./ Inside the car: close
shots of ANNA and GIRL: silence.

The six children run yelling into the house, Agnes trying to
control them.

Cut to TURK's car, arriving in front of the house, a long low
white structure, aggressively modern in design, built on the
shell of an old World War Two fortification./ ANNA gets out
and puts her hand in to help the GIRL, who remains sitting in
the back, loosely playing with her fingers)

ANNA. Come on now. We're home.

(Cut to the central room of TURK's house. A very large,
openplan room, with wide arches to the other living areas.

198

TURK's large study abuts on one end, with a huge window
overlooking the wide flat beach and sea beyond, and the
kitchen-cum-eating area the opposite end. A side arcade
leads to the main entrance and rest of the house./ The building
has massive white walls and glass roofs throughout, giving
a feeling of strength but also of light and spaciousness. Signs
of the origin of the building can be seen - blocked gun ports,
lookout positions and huge recoil pieces let into the floor and
walls./ Except for the study, the whole place is strewn with
toys, books, drawings on the walls, sticks, large seashells,
overcoats, happily flung about.

There are seven children milling noisily around: BRUNO, 6,
gruff, four-square-bottomed: CLARE, 8: PERRY, 10,
earnest and sensitive; VINCENT 12, nearest to his father
in temperament: CATHY, 14, quiet and homely: CRISPIN,
16: and AGNES 18, who is trying to control the pandemonium.

AGNES. Cathy - see what's the matter with Bruno, will you?
Perry - come on, will you? - Perry! - oh Bruno stop that,
stop it! (etc.)

(The main door opens and the children turn and watch in
sudden silence as PETTA - the girl - comes in with TURK
and ANNA)

TURK. Well. Here she is then - the little girl who's going to
live with us.

(Pause. The children stare)

BRUNO. Hallo.

(They all chorus hallo)

PERRY. What's her name?

TURK. She, er, hasn't got a name yet.

VINCENT. Hasn't got a name?

TURK. (crossing away to study area with bundle of papers) Or
we don't know what it is, or was, so we'll have to choose one
later, OK?

(BRUNO walks right up to her and thrusts his face at her
virtually under the blanket)

CATHY. - yes, but she must <u>have</u> one daddy!

199

BRUNO. (as if she hadn't heard the first time) Hallo!

AGNES. Bruno!

BRUNO. She's black!

ANNA. Yes.

BRUNO. She's a black girl!

AGNES. Yes!

BRUNO. (beams delighted) Oh!

(The GIRL flaps her hands aimlessly. The children watch)

PERRY. What's that thing over her head for?

ANNA. It's nothing, just a comfort she has, it'll come off later.

VINCENT. It's blanket, isn't it, a bit of old blanket?

ANNA. Agnes, look after her a minute, will you - there we are...

AGNES. Would she like anything do you think? - some warm
    milk, or -

ANNA. (as she goes) Yes, that's...

CATHY. I'll get it.

(She runs out. The children watch the GIRL, as she wanders,
moving aimlessly towards a window. Silence./ AGNES
crosses to her)

AGNES. There now, come and meet everyone -

CRISPIN. That's no good.

BRUNO. Isn't it, Crispin?

AGNES. Now this is Bruno who said hallo.

BRUNO. Hallo.

AGNES. And this is -

VINCENT. What's the matter with her?

AGNES. Nothing Vincent, it must all be very strange to her that's all - she only arrived yesterday remember.

CRISPIN. And she can't understand English, can she.

BRUNO. Can't she?

PERRY. What would she speak then?

VINCENT. Wugamaloo.

(The children laugh)

AGNES. Vincent. That's silly. Now this is Clare.

(CLARE kisses her)

BRUNO. Wuglamuloo! (laughs)

AGNES. Vincent -

VINCENT. Hallo hallo.

PERRY. Peregrine Godfray, how do you do?

AGNES. - and that's Crispin.

CRISPIN. Look, there's no point, she's not taking the slightest bit of notice.

AGNES. No, but it's...friendly.

PERRY. What's the matter with her?

(The GIRL's eyes wander continuously without fixing on anything: she occasionally flaps her hands or moves her body aimlessly)

AGNES. She's a bit frightened I expect.

PERRY. Of us?

AGNES. Of everything.

BRUNO. Of me. (he growls like a bear)

VINCENT. Of the gull woman, the old gull woman, whooo... !
(he acts a ghostly seagull, bouncing noisily around)

CLARE. Don't Vincent! Vincent!

(CATHY returns with the milk)

CATHY. Here we are.

AGNES. There now -

BRUNO. Drinky up.

(AGNES goes down on her haunches to her)

AGNES. Drink up now, there's a good girl.

(The GIRL stiffens up and averts her gaze as the milk is offered)

Come on now.

(She draws back as AGNES moves the cup nearer her face)

CATHY. Don't - force her.

AGNES. No I won't, I just...

VINCENT. Here, let me.

AGNES. I don't think - Daddy?

TURK. (working, apart) Mm?

AGNES. Look.

VINCENT. Here we are, little girl.

(He holds it up to her face: she pushes it away, not looking properly, but using quick, peripheral glances in his direction)

TURK. Here.

(He takes over the milk, and goes right down to her, offering it to her gently./ She suddenly takes an isolated sip, jerkily, suspiciously: then gives him a short but straight look, fully in the eyes: grabs the cup and drinks ravenously./ She finishes, thrusts the cup back to TURK, turns abruptly away, spilling the last mouthful of milk as she does so)

BRUNO. Careful!

CLARE. (burst) Let's take her outside!

PERRY. Outside?

CATHY. It's too cold -

CRISPIN. Don't be silly.

(CATHY. - for her, too cold coming from a hot country!)
( )
(CLARE. Oh no, come on, we'd run! Down to the sea,)
(come on! - let's take her!) overlapping
( )
(AGNES. Clare, I don't think we should -)
( )
(VINCENT. Hey Dad, it's too cold for her isn't it?)

TURK. No, you go along out, go on the lot of you, scram, scat.

   (Chorus of disapproval from all except CLARE)

CATHY. Well - my old coat -

CRISPIN. Just quick then! -

CLARE. Let's show her the Ark, we'd play on -

(AGNES. Oh no, not that far)
( )
(GRISPIN. I'm not going to that old thing -) sim.
( )
(CATHY. It'd be much too cold, far too cold there -)

CLARE. (topping) Yes we will, yes we will, she'd like it -

AGNES. We won't stay long -

TURK. OK, OK -

PERRY. Come on then, me first -

BRUNO. Look, she's got that thing right over again!

CATHY. Come on little girl.

AGNES. Come on, we won't hurt you -

   (General shout and chatter as they move out. PETTA has
   the blanket right over her head again, almost covering her

203

face. She goes out with great reluctance)

(TURK works, muttering to himself as he goes through the papers)

ANNA. (returning) Have they gone out? (no reply: she wanders over to the window) Getting dark.

TURK. They'll be alright.

ANNA. Mm.

TURK. The best thing is to... just let her adjust herself with the kids, it'll all click then.

ANNA. It's going to be more involved than that.

(Pause. The kids are heard shouting outside)

TURK. Some of these are... (examines photos)

ANNA. Mm?

TURK. Eh?

ANNA. What's so...?

TURK. These prints, they were with the papers that... publicity stuff - you remember the chap that came down here? - (holds one out) Look at that! -

ANNA. Oh.

TURK. (admiration) Oh that's...!

ANNA. Have you noticed - the trouble she has, just walking?

*(The beach. The children, bouncing along in a noisy group across the flat, hard plain of sand, half a mile wide, that is uncovered when the tide is out. CLARE is some way ahead of the group. PERRY hops, BRUNO trots, others throw stones and jump about as they go. The wind is icy. They talk fast and excitedly)

BRUNO. We can teach her things, show her things!

CRISPIN. - watch out! -

VINCENT. What sort of things?

204

BRUNO. Everything! (puffing) Birds, and things, and stones, and sea monsters, you know - (expansive gesture)... the lot!

PERRY. But she'd have seen things like that in her own country, where she comes from, won't she?

VINCENT. No, there's only been fighting there.

AGNES. It's stopped now.

PERRY. Has it?

AGNES. Oh yes, all the fighting's over.

BRUNO. I'll show her elephants and giraffes, and my bicycle, and - and my prickle.

(They round a sanddune)

VINCENT. Look, there's the sea, the sea!

(They all turn to her, excitedly, for a great reaction. She stands, fidgeting and moving her leg aimlessly, her eyes wandering, registering nothing)

CATHY. Perhaps she's seen it before.

CRISPIN. Course she will have.

CATHY. No sea in the middle of Africa, silly.

PERRY. (shouts in her ear) Look - sea!

AGNES. Alright Perry, alright.

(Pause. They look at her, disappointed)

BRUNO. She's not very interested.

PERRY. Is there sea where you're going, Agnes?

AGNES. I don't know where they're sending me yet.

(They all watch the GIRL)

CATHY. (gently) The sea!

(Silence)

CLARE. (who is some way ahead of them) <u>There</u> it is, over

CLARE. (who is some way ahead of them) <u>There</u> it is, over
(here! (shouts) This way!   )
(   ) overlapping
(CRISPIN. Oh, not that, we're not -   )
(   )
(CLARE. There's the Ark, look!   )
(   )
(CATHY. - she won't want to see that.   )
(   )
(AGNES. (shouts) We're not going there Clare - it's too far and)
(too cold!   )

CLARE. (shouts back) Just to <u>show</u> - just to <u>show</u> her!

AGNES. No!

CRISPIN. Only an old landing craft.

VINCENT. It's got ghosts - whoooooo....!

BRUNO. Can she see ghosts, do you think?

CLARE. Yes, but still -

AGNES. <u>No</u>, Clare!

CLARE. Why did we come then? - (they catch her up) - eh?

CRISPIN. Come on, let's get back.

CATHY. What shall we call her?

BRUNO. Who?

CATHY. - er - she - she'll have to have a name.

CLARE. Oh!

(They bounce along in silence for a moment, thinking)

PERRY. Sambo.

CATHY. She's a girl, silly.

PERRY. Alright, you think of one.

CATHY. Jane.

AGNES. Dorothy.

206

VINCENT. Tweedle.

(Pause)

CRISPIN. Griselda.

CATHY. Aphra Jehoshaphat.

CLARE. Emilia Constantine Phiggins, O.M.

BRUNO. Fred.

CATHY. Bert.

PERRY. Bloggs.

CRISPIN. Cloggs.

VINCENT. Number nine!

AGNES. Wheeee!

   *(TURK's study again: TURK places photo against wall. It
   is one of himself, windswept, on a deserted beach, against
   grey sea)

ANNA. Are you going to speak to Agnes before she goes?

TURK. Eh?

ANNA. She's leaving tomorrow, you may not see her again for
   months. You ought to - make it up. (beat) Turk, she goes
   away to start her International Service tomorrow! -

TURK. I'm going to use that, use it for the next campaign - you
   know - Freedom. For the posters, y'know, show it to Glan
   Thursday. (beat) She won't go.

ANNA. (with a sort of helpless incredulity) She's going!

   (TURK switches on a desk light and pulls a thick pile of papers
   towards him./ ANNA picks up a toy from the floor and stands
   there with it. Silence)

   *(The beach. They are just on the edge of the water, CLARE
   and PERRY splashing along in the shallows)

CRISPIN. Whoooo.... (shivers) - it's bleak.

VINCENT. Let's run then.

BRUNO. (imitating CRISPIN) Whoooo!

CLARE. (to GIRL) It's fun, isn't it?

CATHY. Is she warm enough do you think?

VINCENT. She's alright, what about me?

PERRY. - you can't tell, she's so funny.

VINCENT. - anyhow, she'll have to get used to it with Dad
around. (sings loudly and tunelessly) Lala la la la la...

PERRY. He loves it.

AGNES. Well, he was born here too.

CRISPIN. Over there (points)

PERRY. No, that's the school, it's all falling down. He went
to school there, but -

(Longshot of the ruined school seen distantly across the flat
marshes: PERRY points to another spot)

- that's where he was born, there, see? There's a bit of an
old ruined church that was covered by the sea, and masses
of brambles. Used to be a village there.

AGNES. It's very dangerous, don't you ever go near it.

PERRY. Dad's War Memorial board thing, that's from there.

CLARE. What is?

PERRY. That thing over his desk. Names of dead soldiers.

BRUNO. That's where the gull woman lives.

CRISPIN. Ach!....

VINCENT. No, it isn't.

CRISPIN. - no such person!

BRUNO. There is, there is Crispin, I've seen her and she's horrible.

CLARE. Don't Bruno, don't talk about –

BRUNO. She is. She lives out there on the Marsh and she eats raw seagulls alive, and their eggs - she'd eat you up in one go - Crumpp! (he snaps his jaws) She's got horrible big red eyes!

PERRY. (laughs and sings)

VINCENT. (ghost) I'm the gull woman! (he runs about, haunting and howling, eating gulls. Shouts:) Hey - gruppy!

(He points. With a yell, they all rush through the icy water to a fish he has spotted, flapping in the shallows ahead of them. Screams and shouts. CLARE gets there first and grabs it)

VINCENT. Give it me!

CLARE. No - let me!

VINCENT. Let me! -

(With a tremendous flurry of scales and icy water, she gets it and throws it back into the water, screaming with excitement)

*(TURK's study. Silence. ANNA moves about aimlessly, stops)

ANNA. Do you want anything to eat?

TURK. Mm?

(Pause. He works)

ANNA. Food. (pause: deliberately) Are - You - Hungry?

(No reply. Pause. She slowly walks out of the room. Close shot of TURK working, his lips moving)

*(The beach. As they run along shrieking after the fish, PERRY has come across the body of a bird washed up on the sands)

PERRY. Oh! Look! Look!

(They stop abruptly. Silence)

CLARE. (instantly near to tears) Oh! -

CRISPIN. It's a guillemot.

VINCENT. It's dead.

CRISPIN. Or a crested, er...

CATHY. Oh!

(CLARE crouches down to it)

AGNES. Clare - don't -

PERRY. Don't touch it! Don't touch it!

(CLARE gently examines the bird)

BRUNO. It's got fleas.

(CLARE gently opens its wings further and moves its head. /
Pause. / She becomes agitated and tries to make its wings
move. / A completely different atmosphere is overtaking the
children. Their easy well-knit little society has suddenly
disintegrated into icyness and isolation at the fact of death)

CATHY. (shivers) Cold.

(Bird cries overhead. They look up. / A great cloud of
seagulls wheeling above them in disorder)

CRISPIN. Hey! Clare!

(CLARE is running away from the spot, very fast, in a dead
straight line along the water's edge)

AGNES. Clare!

(VINCENT pushes the bird with his foot: it rolls over. They
stare at it with fascinated repulsion. Gull cries overhead. /
Cut to: the remains of a wartime landing craft, half buried in
the sand and almost rusted away. Snow has drifted against
it. / CLARE runs straight to it, with her tight, intense, fast
run. She climbs onto the top. / Cut to: the interior. She
crouches into a hole in the craft and curls up. It is just big
enough for her. Strange stones and seashells she has collected
are stored in little nooks in the walls around her.

Cut to: closeshot TURK working, muttering to himself: photo

and papers: then pan up to the board mounted on the wall above his head - the 1914-18 war memorial board from Old Romney church - now broken and worn as if it had been many years in the open air. It is fixed on the wall over TURK's desk.

Mix to: ANNA lying on her bed, eyes open.

Cut to: VINCENT whirling the dead bird round his head and casting it out to sea. The children stand side by side, silent, and watch it drift in the water. / Cut to the GIRL, standing there temporarily forgotten, stock still, her clothes blowing in the icy wind. / Cut to the children watching the drifting bird. / Cut to the GIRL: her face suddenly lights up as if with tremendous delight, and she flaps her hands quickly, almost ecstatically. Then, after a moment, she abruptly gives way to an appalling despair, her head back and arms out like a scarecrow, sounding little panting moans, just audible, and rocking her head from side to side in desperation. Fade)

(Fade up: Helicopter in flight. Bright sunlight. Inside it: CELLY and GLANVILLE)

CELLY. There!

GLANVILLE. My God!

CELLY. What?

GLANVILLE. I'd forgotten! Bleak, flat...

CELLY. Oh! - ha! - I love it.

GLANVILLE. Yes, well, I suppose you can get used to anything.

(Film of Dengemarsh from the air, broad and sunny)

And you were brought up down here?

CELLY. Since I was ten, when they brought me back to England with them.

GLANVILLE. Yes...

CELLY. You'd think being born in the Philippines, that's what I'd

want. But - nope! (she grins broadly) Look - there's the
lighthouse, see?

GLANVILLE. And what are those?

CELLY. Atomic Power Station.

GLANVILLE. But no - people, no houses, look at it!

CELLY. It's a nature reserve, ours is the only house.

GLANVILLE. Appropriate.

CELLY. The sea used to cover all this. But now it's going out
again - ten, twenty feet a year. Something to do with
shingle being washed up by the Channel currents or something, making more land. Gee! - we used to see it like
this when we came back at weekends - be in London all the
week, me at school of course, but Turk and Anna working
flat out starting Campaign, 18-hour days Monday to
Saturday. We'd come down here Sunday morning very
early, six or seven maybe - just like this, the sun right
across the Marshes, everything fresh and green - but they'd
not stop talking all the way, they were so _involved_ in it all...
there's the house, see, over there on the right... and,
oh! - (suddenly like a child) - look, look at the sea!

GLANVILLE. But when you're sixty-something -

CELLY. He's not sixty.

GLANVILLE. No?

CELLY. Fifty-seven, fifty-eight, I think.

GLANVILLE. Oh? Anyhow, that's a pace that can't be kept up,
right? - without something going very wrong, even if you're
well to start with.

CELLY. Have you tried stopping him?

GLANVILLE. Huh!

CELLY. And?

GLANVILLE. (grunts and shrugs)

CELLY. (grins)

GLANVILLE. You can't...

CELLY. What?

GLANVILLE. - see clearly any more. When you get like that.

(Pause)

CELLY. I'm going to try and get him to let me have a good look
at him while we're there. He just won't see a doctor
normally, you know. Something'll have to be done. He
must - accept...

GLANVILLE. Mm?

CELLY. (beat) He spent most of his life fighting and battering
his way through to finding out what he could do; and once
he'd found it, there's just been no stopping him.

GLANVILLE. Ignoring what he doesn't want to know about - like
you joining the U.N. Children's Department -

CELLY. Three years it took him to accept that. "Disloyal"!

GLANVILLE. Fantastic.

CELLY. Agnes is going through it now. It'll happen to all the
kids, too, one by one, as they... "desert him", ha!

GLANVILLE. The last of the dinosaurs. You know what gets me?
- his absolute steaming arrogance! So absolutely bloody
sure of himself, there's just no doubts!

CELLY. (smile) No?

GLANVILLE. How-ever...

CELLY. Mm?

GLANVILLE. - this - (holding up a file) - will change all that.

CELLY. What's that?

GLANVILLE. The adoption figures. All those little Malawi
kids.

213

CELLY. (glancing round at him) Yes?

GLANVILLE. (raises his eyebrows eloquently and whistles)

  *(TURK's house. The kids, except for AGNES who does not
  reappear, are playing noisily. / GLANVILLE watches TURK,
  as he stares at the figures in the file. They are in the
  study area)

TURK. What's... (he shakes his head)... what?...

GLANVILLE. Search me chum.

TURK. I mean, it's...there's a mistake, int there? - There
must be.

GLANVILLE. I, er -

TURK. You're not saying...

GLANVILLE. - Don't think so. (he watches him) There's more
applications coming in, of course, but the first rush is over, -

TURK. Yes, well it's only been a few days yet -

GLANVILLE. - but if you knock off a rough third as being
unsuitable one way or another, then -

TURK. What do you mean, unsuitable?

GLANVILLE. What? Well you can't just let any old Tom, Dick
or Harry who asks for one have a child -

TURK. You mean you're...

GLANVILLE. - like a sort of Free Gift over Four Gallons.

TURK. - <u>screening</u> them in some way?

GLANVILLE. Well of course we are!

  (Pause)

TURK. I said <u>every</u> family, <u>every</u> one, not just the -

(GLANVILLE. But it's all in the blueprint, didn't you read) simul-
  the blueprint of the scheme? (picks it up from TURK's)

214

```
(    desk)                                                    )  ⌐
(                                                             )  |
(TURK.  - not just the ones you and your friends approve      )  taneously
(    of.  You let me stand up there in front of the whole -   )
```

GLANVILLE. (topping) Look, man, you don't really care a
    hoot, do you? - so long as you can sit down here dreaming up
    your grand designs, and not be bothered with too much -

TURK. I have to look at the whole thing long term, someone
    has to see -

GLANVILLE. But as I'm the one that has to make it work, me,
    surely you could -

TURK. - can't be tied down to every petty detail that -

GLANVILLE. (topping) Such as people, you mean.

TURK. (beat - angry) I stood up there in front of the whole
    world, and -

GLANVILLE. How is she, by the way?

TURK. What?

GLANVILLE. The little girl.

TURK. (slaps down file and turns away)

GLANVILLE. (angry) Eh?

    (The LITTLE GIRL, on the rocking horse, her head forward
    against the mane, blanket over her head. More of her face
    is visible. / She rocks quietly, steadily, in the centre of the
    room)

ANNA. (watching) She does that by the hour. Just - rocking.

CELLY. With her head forward like that?

ANNA. Yes. There are other things too. With her fingers - like
    this (she mimes a 'milking' gesture, but flutters her
    fingers) She sat on the floor over there and kept it up for
    two hours yesterday. And looking at her hands, too, so
    oddly, and holding them out, like that - as if they didn't belong
    to her.

                                                            215

CELLY. She must have been examined though, when she -

ANNA. I think it was rushed through in time for the - y'know -

CELLY. Yes.

ANNA. - meeting, rally, the big appearance.

   (They watch)

CELLY. What else?

ANNA. She won't look at you.

CELLY. (silence)

ANNA. Her eyes sort of... wander away, like bubbles in a
   spirit level. And if you cuddle her, she just - hangs limp.
   I don't feel she's - retarded, just... I don't know. I have a
   feeling that it's some sort of blockage - it's all happening
   inside, it's all there, only...

   (The other children play noisily around her, but PETTA
   remains steadily rocking, locked in her own silent
   'aloneness')

GLANVILLE. There's another thing. The doctors at the
   Centre -

TURK. (abrupt) What?

GLANVILLE. I'm telling you, just listen, eh? Some of these
   kids have got - something wrong.

TURK. What sort of thing?

GLANVILLE. Sort of... disturbance, they don't know what yet.

TURK. Disturbance?

GLANVILLE. I've been watching your... (gesture)

TURK. How many of them?

GLANVILLE. Could be up to a third.

TURK. (stares at him)

216

GLANVILLE. Of course, it may be nothing, but still -

TURK. Oh, they'll be alright.

GLANVILLE. (firm) - there's something there, though. We can't fix up any that show signs of it. So... (he holds up file: beat) Your kid alright?

(Pause)

TURK. (brisk) Anyhow, look, I asked you down here to -

(GLANVILLE. No, just a minute -)
( )
(TURK. (producing fat file) Yes, well, I've been working)
(it out for a long time, working on it -)
( ) overlapping
(GLANVILLE. You're incredible, you know that? -)
(absolutely bloody -)
( )
(TURK. - the biggest thing, the best scheme that -)
( )
(GLANVILLE. We were talking about this - alright?)
((flourishes file) - and her mates, eh?)

TURK. Oh, that'll be alright.

GLANVILLE. (beat) What d'you mean, that'll be alright?

TURK. It'll sort itself out. But this -

GLANVILLE. No, wait, look -

TURK. (suddenly hard at him) It's your job - didn't you say, you said, didn't you? - your job to make that work. All right then!

GLANVILLE. (shakes his head incredulously)

(TURK. Now this is completely different to anything)
(we've ever done before -)
( ) simultan-
(GLANVILLE. No - no - look -)
( )
(TURK. I want to go through the whole thing -)
( )
(GLANVILLE. Listen will you! -)
( )

217

(TURK. - with you, just straight through once -)
(   ) -eously
(GLANVILLE. Will you listen!   )

    (PETTA rocking steadily, the scrap of blanket over her head)

CELLY. (close) Petta? Do you remember me? Petta?

    (No response. The rocking continues without pause)

    (in Swahili: Remember me do you Petta? Why don't you talk to me?)

CLARE. She doesn't talk, ever.

    (They watch her rocking)

    It's as if she doesn't trust us.

    (CELLY claps her hands sharply one side of PETTA's head)

CLARE. Can she -

CELLY. Shush.

ANNA. Turk - look! Turk!

TURK. (in study area) Eh?

    (CELLY claps her hand the other side. No response)

CLARE. Is it... (she indicates the blanket) ...?

    (CELLY gently reaches out for the blanket. As she touches it, the rocking becomes tense, and then stops)

    Daddy did -

CELLY. Shuch! (pause)

CLARE. (whisper) Daddy did that yesterday, and she looked at him.

ANNA. Looked at him?

    (CELLY slowly removes her hand. Slowly the rocking picks up again, until it is regular, as before)

218

GLANVILLE. If I can't get through to you on this - (file) -
then... Look, this is it, man, there can't be another
campaign, and -

TURK. I don't want to -

GLANVILLE. No, shut it, listen, will you! Because we're not
going to be here next year, do I have to spell it out for you?
- Celly's told you, I've told you... Our functions, all our
functions, are being taken over.

TURK. ... not people!

GLANVILLE. Five years ago the U.N. set up a huge department
with every facility you could think of for massive relief
everywhere in the world - they've got everything man, and in
twelve months they'll have done more good than all the
outfits like ours have done the whole of their existences.
And why? - they've got the lolly man - two per cent of all
national defence budgets - think of that! The General
Assembly took three minutes to vote that - three minutes -
more money than Oxfam, War on Want and all the rest of
us had raised in twenty-five years! That's what you're
fighting.

TURK. But it's not people...

GLANVILLE. What is it then, brass monkeys? Look, with our
set-up, we can only scratch at it - look at the size of it,
man! And look - look at your girl there, look at her! -
that's half the world!

(PETTA rocks)

CELLY. Look at that -

(CATHY and PERRY are singing, more or less absentmindedly
as they play, a simple little tune of five notes or so, with a
regular beat)

ANNA. What?

CELLY. She's keeping time to it.

(PETTA is rocking in time. The tune changes, and after a
moment of uncertainty, the rhythm of the rocking changes
and comes into line. PETTA is completely hidden under
the blanket. BRUNO comes roaring in)

BRUNO. Mummy, mummy, look what Vincent did to my lorry, look - (etc.)

ANNA. Quiet Bruno, alright, shush, shut up... (etc.)

(The singing stops. PETTA gets off the horse, disjointedly, aimlessly, and starts to meander across the room, legs spread wide out and kept stiff at the knee, rocking from side to side, so she moves forward in great gawky jerks, flapping her hands. The other kids run noisily about the room./ CELLY starts to la-la the first tune. After a moment, PETTA, whose back is towards her, begins to move rhythmically to it./ She crosses the room, keeping in time, so that her movement is almost like a loose dance, until she comes to the study area./ There she stops abruptly and looks straight and clear at TURK, her face shiningly clear and intelligent, a sudden startling island of normality)

ANNA. (in an urgent whisper) Turk! Turk!

(PETTA turns abruptly away, jerky and grotesque again. The island has gone.)

(TURK is showing GLANVILLE the photo he chose the previous day)

TURK. This, you see, the main billing -

GLANVILLE. The what?

TURK. The posters, and the theme, you know, on all the publicity -

GLANVILLE. ...off a duck's back!'.

TURK. And the layout of each one -

GLANVILLE. Look, we've got to cope with these (file) somehow! - got to think what to do!

TURK. (stops dead, licking his lips)

GLANVILLE. Maybe we should... think about shifting gear a bit.

TURK. (quickly) You go on bringing them over, it'll be alright.

(Pause)

220

GLANVILLE. What do you mean, it'll be alright? - How can we -

TURK. Look, leave it all to me, alright? - I know what I'm about.

GLANVILLE. Well just drop me a little hint will you? After all, -

TURK. (quickly) We'll give it a week.

(Pause)

GLANVILLE. We'll what?

TURK. Then you'll see. People don't just... stop being people. The homes'll come, you'll see.

(Pause)

GLANVILLE. And the other business?

TURK. Mm?

GLANVILLE. The illness?

(TURK stands blank)

    *(TURK's bedroom, 1 a.m. ANNA is in bed: TURK restless
    at the window. / The flash of the lighthouse sweeps the room,
    flooding it with light every twenty seconds)

TURK. (muttering) Must... (pressing his fist on the glass)...
    stop... (staccato) Yes, yes.

ANNA. Talk about it, eh?

TURK. Mm?

ANNA. Talk to me about it.

TURK. It's a temporary, er, holdup, or something.

(Pause)

ANNA. You don't think -

TURK. It'll happen, though, people don't just - change, not
    like this anyway.

ANNA. How do you know? -

TURK. Yes. Yes.

ANNA. - you just believe what you want to believe.

> (Pause. The lighthouse sweeps the room. TURK mutters)

> Turk listen. You know what could happen? -

TURK. (silence)

ANNA. - what could come out of all this? - we could, some life of our own.

> (Pause)

TURK. (nodding sarcastically) You mean if -

ANNA. We had some once, didn't we? - when we were starting it all, the first campaign, working like stink every hour round the clock - the kids starting to grow, it was nonstop, bang, bang bang -

TURK. It was hell.

ANNA. It was alive, I was alive, part of it, part of you, I mattered. But now I've just... (shrug) ... run out of being needed.

TURK. And you want to -

ANNA. Not go back, you can't go back.

TURK. Well then?

> (Pause)

ANNA. If I were to go, would it make any difference?

TURK. Look, I've got enough on my plate -

ANNA. No, I mean it, I'm serious.

TURK. (beat) What do you mean, 'go'? - what, just...

ANNA. - walk out, yes, go away somewhere.

TURK. Eh? Well... what about the kids, and -

222

ANNA. Oh they're quite self sufficient, got their own rules - they don't need me. We've always planned it that way.

TURK. Ach.

ANNA. - I haven't been such a marvellous mum. (beat) Well?

TURK. Look, just leave me alone for -

ANNA. But what am I doing here? - you tell me, eh? I wake up in the mornings and... I'm 48, do you realise that, and I'm doing nothing!

TURK. (staccato, miles away) Yes. Yes. Yes.

ANNA. Sweet Jesus, your own little world! (Pause. The lighthouse beam sweeps the room. TURK raises and lowers his fist against the glass of the window) Baffled old man.

TURK. (staccato) Yes. Yes.

ANNA. You suddenly remind me of someone. That man you told me about.

TURK. Eh?

ANNA. Used to live here. Mr. Williams, wasn't it? - Old'un?

TURK. (stares at her)

ANNA. Yes. Him. Ha!

TURK. My dad's foreman, ran the farm. He was an old man, not like... he was old.

ANNA. Oh, the world turns.

TURK. (stares at her)

ANNA. He couldn't understand why either, didn't you say?

TURK. You're being bloody stupid, woman. He was an old man, not just... (angry) That's got nothing to do with it!

(There is a tiny movement at the door)

TURK. I fought with him because he was... he'd had it, and -

ANNA. Shush - look -

223

TURK. (very angry) - nothing, nothing to do with it!

ANNA. (points)

TURK. What?

(Tiny movement at the door. TURK makes to cross to it)

ANNA. No - Turk - (The door opens, slowly. PETTA stands
there, in her nightclothes, the blanket round her shoulders)
Petta? Are you alright darling? Petta? (PETTA comes
quickly into the room) What is it darling? Do you want something? Eh? Come here Petta. (PETTA moves sharply,
clumsily, seemingly in a haphazard fashion, towards ANNA. /
She stops centre of the room, and starts repeating the
'milking' gesture, over and over, but much faster than usual,
and with little whimpers of distress, as if labouring with an
internal and invisible stress. / The lighthouse beam sweeps
the room) She's trying to reach us Turk - trying to get through.
What is it, what is it eh darling?

(ANNA crosses and goes down to her)

Listen Petta, look at me -

(She passes her hands in front of her eyes. PETTA momentarily follows the movement, then drifts away again)

She can feel us Turk, I know she can... She's not silly, are
you darling, just that... something's in the way, isn't it?

(PETTA repeats the milking gesture, getting faster, giving
funny little panting-sighing noises)

How can we... what can we... she's just here, so close, if
only we could... get through somehow - how can we - oh!...

(Suddenly, with a great shriek, PETTA turns and runs at
TURK in the far corner of the room. / She grabs one of
his hands, clutching it tight to her, and kicks, scratches,
bites, hits, bangs, butts him all at once, screaming and
screaming appallingly. / ANNA has run with her, and holds
her tight and lovingly through all this)

(ANNA. That's it darling, good girl, that's it, we're) simul-
(here, we're here -   )

224

(TURK. Hey - stop it - what the - what do you em -) ─┐
(ouch, ugh -   ) taneously
(   )
(PETTA. (screaming)   ) ─┘

ANNA. Don't reject her, help her! Shut up you great baby, look
at her, look! We're here darling, we're here!

(PETTA lams into him. He grins his teeth and holds on.
She kicks and hits and bites him, screaming without pause.
Fade)

(A helicopter on the beach, the blades revolving slowly. A
man climbs aboard and it roars into full power.

Inside TURK's house, in the main living area. TURK and
ANNA are at it hammer and tongs: PETTA sits there. As
the scene opens, the helicopter flies off over the house)

TURK. Look, I can't, can I? - I mean, how can I?

(ANNA. When we took her on -   ) ─┐
(   ) overlapping
(TURK. When we took her on, it never occurred to us   )
(that this sort of thing could -   )
(   )
(ANNA. No qualifications, you said, no strings, just   )
(open your arms and give them homes no matter what -   )
(   )
(TURK. But it's a highly specialised business working with   )
(a - what did he call her?   ) ─┘

ANNA. He didn't actually -

TURK. Yes, I know, but there was a word, a word he used -

ANNA. Autism.

TURK. Yes, well, even he said it wasn't understood properly...
and I know nothing about it, nothing, how can I? Look, I'm
sorry little girl, but you'll have to go back to your mates.

ANNA. If she does -

TURK. Oh she will, she's got to, we can't -

ANNA. If she does, there'd be the publicity - everyone else will

225

start to do the same; and you know what that'll mean.

TURK. (frantic) Yes, but she can't stay here, can she? - needs expert care and -

ANNA. The best thing, he _said_, didn't he _say_? - the best thing is to -

TURK. Let her live with the kids, yes.

ANNA. Just let her be with the kids, have... normal kids around her while she's having treatment.

TURK. Yes, but...

ANNA. Ha!

TURK. - it's this business of -

ANNA. - _attaching_ herself to _you_! -

TURK. Look, I just haven't got the time!

ANNA. Why not?

TURK. Why not? I've got to put every ounce I've got into... got to give every second to _stopping_... to somehow _stop_...

(He has come face to face with PETTA: stops for a moment: then quickly turns away, switching his tack to:)

This illness, it's a sort of blockage; kids that have it have a high IQ, but there's something blocking their communication with people - that's what he said.

ANNA. Right.

TURK. So they sort of fix on someone - lock themselves onto someone, and that's it mate, you become her...

ANNA. Her sort of everything.

TURK. Her... (gestures)

(He walks rapidly up and down)

And I'd have to do _everything_ for her, sort of live with her day and night for months, talk to her, feed her, and if she reacts like he said she might... change her bleeding -

ANNA. Yes!

TURK. Eh? And what for?

ANNA. For her.

TURK. Eh?

(He catches PETTA's eye as she sits there, watching him)

(shout) Oh...

(ANNA unexpectedly smiles at him)

TURK. (suddenly bangs the table and yells) ...pigs!

(Quick shot: TURK unceremoniously dressing PETTA, almost
throwing her clothes on./ Quick shot: TURK getting her to use
a spoon to eat, getting in an awful mess ./ Quick shot: TURK
scrubbing her teeth with fury.

The beach: TURK and PETTA walking along the water's edge,
TURK with his hands full of 'treasures' - bits of shells and
seaweed that PETTA keeps finding and passing to him
to hold)

TURK. (angry mutter) Why me, eh? - why did it have to be me?
I mean, look at the choice - you can't move in my house for
kids. There's Cathy, now Cathy, she'd have been terrific
for you, but - Oh No. (more treasures) Look, no more,
eh? - that's enough. Or Perry, Perry's a nice little boy,
why can't you go after him? -

(Corner of kitchen/ eating area: TURK feeding her)

- it's not as if I can give you the time, see, I'm a - a
public figure, and there's a crisis. Because everything's...
(suddenly like a tearful child)... it's all falling apart, you
see, and if you knew how much I've put into it all, everything
I am... not in your hair! - ugh...ach! With your spoon for
God's sake -

(Flat roof of house: she is stacking toy blocks. The kids also
there)

- and anyhow, you're sick, and it's not my job just because
you happen to have picked on me, to... (pleading to her)
There isn't enough known about this thing, and that's not my

fault, is it? You should be in a hospital or... no, look, on
top of each other see, like this (CRISPIN passes more
blocks) Aw stop it Crispin for God's sake -

CRISPIN. I was only -

TURK. I know, I know what you're doing, don't I? (he collides
with BRUNO and PERRY, who fall and yell) Oh sorry,
look I didn't see you, sorry - (he steps on toy plane) Oh
blast and bloody buggeration (howls from BRUNO) I'll buy
you a new one, all right...

(Mix to: PETTA, alone on huge flat beach. Weirdy music.
She stands quite still, seen a long way off. Music continues
under:

TURK's house. TURK is trying to work. The children are
playing ring o' roses with PETTA. They move solemnly
round)

CHILDREN.
Ring a ring of roses
A pocket full of posies
Atishoo, atishoo,
We all fall down!

(They all fall except PETTA, who remains standing, looking
at TURK.

Mix to: Dengemarsh. Music continues under: TURK and
PETTA seen at great distances across the flat, bleak marsh.
TURK impatient, PETTA meandering and curious./ They
start rabbits and hares, which dash away across the shingle
and gorse./ They pass wrecked and rusty ironwork and
shellholes, old leftover fortifications from the war strewn
widely around./Hand in hand, they pass by the huge pylons,
singing away their one strange note in the wind, the massive
lowering piles of the nuclear power station and the lighthouse
beyond./ They pass the skeleton of a large bird: PETTA
stares at it until TURK pulls her away./ They pass the wooden
prow of an old boat, half grown over with brambles and moss:
rusty shellcases almost gone, old scaffolding, an ivymassed
pillbox, fallen away: strange survivals of the war in a dead
country.
Away across the marsh, TURK sees a small BLACK FIGURE
watching him, in a clump of gorse near the ruins of Old
Romney./ He stops, with PETTA by the hand, and stares at
it. /THE FIGURE stands still, regarding him./Gulls wheel
and cry around his head.

228

Mix to: the children's bedroom. Night. PETTA lies
awake, eyes open. The other children sleep.

Mix to: TURK's bedroom. TURK lies awake. ANNA
sleeps. Gulls outside.

Slow mix to: PETTA sitting solitary, the blanket round
her shoulders, lifting and dropping a pebble time after time,
with mechanical repetition.

The main room of TURK's house. CLARE and PERRY
watch her, from another part of the room)

CLARE. Look.

PERRY. Yes.

CLARE. She can't...

PERRY. It's a pebble.

CLARE. ..get through.

(Pause)

She's got to become like a little baby again, that's what Celly
said. When she grew up before, she couldn't...take things
in, she's got a sort of barrier, so she's got to go through it
all again.

PERRY. What, be a baby again?

CLARE. Yes.

PERRY. But you can't do that, it's silly, it's impossible.

CLARE. No. In her mind.

PERRY. Oh. (beat) Is she mad then?

CLARE. (gently) No, not mad.

(They watch her, lifting and dropping the pebble endlessly)

PERRY. Dad's mad, isn't he?

CLARE. He's what?

PERRY. Course he is. He's potty, bad as her.

229

CLARE. What do you mean, mad?

PERRY. Haven't you heard him, talking to himself? Great
long conversations he has when he goes out walking,
shouting and everything; or sometimes in his study there
in the middle of the night. I've woken up and heard it, it's
creepy.

CLARE. What does he talk about?

PERRY. Oh, things. Getting old and that. He doesn't sleep,
you know; neither of them sleep.

(Cut to TURK, standing as if caught mid-thought, miles
away, lips moving)

How can she become like a little baby again?

CLARE. She's got to feel how it all...fits together.

PERRY. What does?

CLARE. Oh, everything... (her face clouds)... except...

(Pause. Gulls cry outside. CLARE shivers)

PERRY. Dad too?

CLARE. (after a pause) Yes.

PERRY. He's not so bad now though is he? Since <u>she</u> came.

(TURK breaks off his dream and looks across at PETTA.
She endlessly drops and picks up the pebble, mechanically,
on and on.

Slow mix to:

*The sea's edge. Shallow waves gliding in)

CLARE. (voice over)...all sorts of fish and seabirds, shells
and rocks and seaweeds, and all the old drowned people,
singing under the sea.

PERRY. What drowned people?

CLARE. All there are, you can hear them singing, they sing.
(beat) And these are shells, Petta -

230

(Panning round to the seven kids coming along the edge of the water. The tide is right out, leaving the flat wide plain of sand./ CRISPIN walks ahead of the others, playing ducks and drakes with stones. CATHY has PETTA by the hand./ CLARE, PERRY and VINCENT search for shells and things, and give them to PETTA./ BRUNO walks behind the others, stamping on things with his large boots and examining the effect./ The kids are scattered, not grouped, moving along towards the old landing craft. In the distance behind them can be seen the huge grey ghostly hulks of the nuclear power station)

- tiny fish make them and live in them, under the water, -

CRISPIN. Come on!

CATHY. Alright.

CRISPIN. Look at that kid.

PERRY. Bruno!

BRUNO. (puffing) Coming.

CLARE. - they live inside there, see?

VINCENT. Have you told Dad yet?

CRISPIN. No.

PERRY. He won't like it.

CRISPIN. (throwing) I don't see why.

CATHY. You know why. He doesn't like the U.N. or anything like that. He says it's not people.

VINCENT.)
PERRY.)   (derisive)!
CRISPIN.)

CATHY. Now that's enough. He's got some funny, old-fashioned values, but you shouldn't laugh at them.

CRISPIN. (throwing a stone) I'm going to join them anyway.

CLARE. (to PETTA)...and this is popweed, you lie it in the

sun then after it's dry you can pop it with your fingers...
pop! - see? (she laughs, and sings a sudden snatch of tune)

VINCENT. But what about, you know - your International
Service?

CRISPIN. This is instead. If you join any of these U.N.
Departments you get exemption. Same work really.

CATHY. Oh.

PERRY. I'm going to India for mine.

CATHY. That'll be in... (she calculates)...1983.

PERRY. That's right.

VINCENT. What will you do there?

PERRY. Oh, the famine work.

CRISPIN. They'll have fed everyone by then.

PERRY. Will they?

CRISPIN. - it'll all be medical stuff, and teaching about growing
and how to irrigate, that sort of thing.

BRUNO. (puffing up) If I irrigate, I scratch.

CLARE. ...no, this foot, see, the first foot, now, as I - (she
sings a snatch of tune) - up, like this (she dances a step)...

CATHY. Come on Clare.

VINCENT. She's so quiet.

CRISPIN. Petta?

PERRY. She doesn't sleep at all, just lies there, all night,
eyes open.

VINCENT. It's how you're born.

PERRY. Is it?

VINCENT. There are babies born at operations, you know; they
cut the mother open and lift it out -

(CATHY. Ugh, don't Vincent!)
(   ) simultaneously
(BRUNO. Do they?   )

VINCENT. - and they grow up calm people, and often sort of
weak and placid.

CATHY. That's not true!

VINCENT. It is true, I've read about it!

CATHY. But it's not usual, is it? Most babies are born,
well...

VINCENT. - they have to sort of struggle. The more the baby
has to fight to get out, the stronger it'll be.

PERRY. What about the mother?

VINCENT. Sometimes she suffers terribly if the baby is strong.

CLARE. It's good though, it's a good thing.

VINCENT. Being born's the most violent thing that ever happens
to you, did you know that? - the most violent thing in your
whole life -

CLARE. (sings a snatch of tune)

VINCENT. - and the babies that have to fight and scramble their
way out - they're tough, they're somebody.

CLARE. Come on, right up, this foot, look like this - (she
sings)... la la la...

BRUNO. (sudden shout) Hey!

(Still keeping up the shout, he runs ahead. The others join in
and follow, to the old landing craft. BRUNO immediately
clambers up onto it)

CATHY. Careful Bruno.

CRISPIN. (climbing up) In my young days it was pretty well

233

complete. Rusty, but... there was a room inside.

CLARE. There is, there is still -

(They are all clambering and jumping over it. CRISPIN is excited again as he was when he was younger)

CRISPIN. - haven't been here for ages!

PERRY. Only this little one.

CRISPIN. - look, it's rusting away!

(BRUNO starts firing an imaginary machine gun)

CLARE. See the little room, Petta? Look, see, in there. Look, you can see through this hold - a little room!

BRUNO. What was it used for Crispin?

CRISPIN. Oh, it's an old landing craft, they used them in the Second World War.

(BRUNO escalates to a tremendous assault by air which he beats off single handed)

CRISPIN. - landing soldiers and that during an invasion.

CLARE. It's the Ark, the Ark, all the animals!

(VINCENT drums his heels against the side of the craft: it makes a terrific din)

CATHY. Stop it Vincent! - Bruno! - you'll frighten her!

CRISPIN. (jumping about) Look, see, these are shellholes through the walls. It was used for target practice one time.

VINCENT. Watch her - look -

(PETTA is clambering up to the top of the craft)

CLARE. She's alright.

CATHY. (fingers in ears) It's dangerous!

BRUNO. Did they have big guns too, Crispin?

CRISPIN. I think so!

234

CLARE. It's the Ark, the animals! The sea used to come right up to here - but now it's going out, it's going out...

(BRUNO continues his colossal assault, now assisted by artillery. VINCENT shouts and sings, banging his heels against the hull for extra effect)

CATHY. Don't Vincent - Crispin stop him - you'll frighten her.

PERRY. Look out down there - watch out for us!

CRISPIN. (throwing stones high into the air, shouting over the din) I - can - hit - the - sky!

CATHY. Stop it! Stop it! Clare - Petta! -

(CLARE jumps down into the hole.

Cut to the interior - the tiny room, just big enough to get into. The noise is suddenly very strange down here - a hollow booming, as if in a huge dark tunnel, very loud. PETTA lies curled up in a bundle, completely covered with her blanket)

CLARE. Petta? Petta?

(She moves the blanket and for the first time it comes away without protest. PETTA lies there, curled up foetally, her face streaming with tears, but quite silent and still. Motionless)

PERRY. (outside - shouts) Here we come! Here we come!

(The din inside is colossal, hurting the ears)

  *(Cut to: Closeshot a bloodied arm, bandages being removed. The arm is CELLY's, and we are in TURK's house)

GLANVILLE. Yow!

CELLY. It's alright.

GLANVILLE. Any splinters in it, any glass?

(ANNA. What was this? - here I'll just -   ) over-
(   )
(GLANVILLE. Flaming madman -   )

(CELLY. Nothing, I couldn't see.   )
(   )
(ANNA. - wash it first.   ) -lapping
(   )
(CELLY. Nothing to worry about!   )

GLANVILLE. Didn't you see? - didn't you see it on the telly?

ANNA. We don't have -

GLANVILLE. Fantastic, right along the Strand and up to St.
     Paul's, all the Barbican...one woman I saw had a cut right
     across here, blood pouring down. But it was the broken
     windows that really -

ANNA. But what, who was this?

GLANVILLE. The crowds, love, just people walking about, not
     knowing what to do with themselves. Most of them, their
     working week's been cut to half in a year - only do twenty
     hours or so now.

ANNA. But what -?

GLANVILLE. Automation, see? Been creeping up on us for
     years now, but suddenly... bingo! - streets are full of them,
     someone breaks a window, a fight starts...all those anaemic
     commuters, remember? - the 8.13 to Cannon Street and
     all that? - marauding bloody lions, love, they can't take it,
     don't know what to do with themselves. It's all just starting
     to crack open like a gigantic egg - and all over, not just little
     old London. They're not educated for Life - just for
     some miserable mean little job...we've been waiting so long
     to learn what life's all for, and managed to avoid it for so
     long - but now it's starting, just starting to... where's
     your old man?

ANNA. Washing nappies.

     (TURK enters, in apron)

TURK. ...all over again, that's the second time tonight she's -
     (sees them and stops)

CELLY. Hallo Turk.

GLANVILLE. Hallo.

TURK. Look at these - (soiled nappies) - how can I be expected
236

to work when every hour or so...

(He stops and looks at them again)

GLANVILLE. I've, er, got some figures here. (holds up a file)

(Pause)

TURK. Yes, I see.

ANNA. I didn't think - I didn't know they were coming, Turk.

CELLY. Yes, I'm sorry we -

TURK. Doesn't matter.

GLANVILLE. ...thought it might be better if we just came.

(Pause)

TURK. Yes, well. (he looks at the file under GLANVILLE's arm)

(Pause)

ANNA. Let's eat anyway.

*(Later. The four round the table. Nothing has been eaten)

TURK. (speaking very fast) You should see her hands - they've got these very fine veins, you know, just under the skin, terribly fine. And just in the last few days, the way she moves around, you know, it's got - just that bit smoother, know what I mean? - how she used to be all gawky?

CELLY. Yes, I know.

GLANVILLE. But - it's only been -

TURK. - a very little time, I know, I know, but it's started, you can see it's just started to come right - not dramatic or anything, but you can see a - a - sort of beginning.

GLANVILLE. Yes, well...

(He places the file carefully on the table. Silence. TURK pulls out the fossil round his neck and grips it. The sea is heard outside)

TURK. (the dam starting to burst at last) You know you can spend
   your life, your whole life, fighting and slogging and bashing
   your way through, trying to do something, trying to achieve
   something... but what is there? - that you can do? - when
   it comes to it - that makes any difference, any real
   difference, to anything at all, you tell me! And you think -
   why did I bother, eh? - where's it all gone, all the years,
   the years of it...

GLANVILLE. (gently) I know how you -

TURK. No you don't, you don't know...double-first and face
   smooth as a pig's arse, you know? I spent twenty years
   finding out what it was about, even - twenty years before -

GLANVILLE. And you know now?

TURK. I know more than you'll ever know about it son, I'll
   tell you that -

ANNA. Turk, I don't think -

TURK. You never fought for it, did you? I mean, really?
   Never held a gun?

GLANVILLE. No.

TURK. Well I have -

GLANVILLE. Yes.

TURK. - and I've looked at people, talked to people that were
   dying, son -

GLANVILLE. I'm sure you have.

TURK. - killed fighting for something, you know - they might
   not be bloody intellectuals, and they might have only a very
   confused idea of what it was all about, but they were fighting
   for something they felt in their... (bangs his belly)...laying
   down their lives -

GLANVILLE. (embarrassed) Yes, OK, we haven't all been so -

TURK. I've held a man that had the bottom half of him just not
   there any longer, you know that? And he just looked at me -
   and his face, his face...
238 That's what counts son, that's what hurts - so that when

you close your eyes for a minute or stop what you're doing, that face comes up - no, not the face, the eyes, just the eyes, the look, you forget the face even. And it's like all the blokes you ever knew that got killed - and the ones you didn't know - like that, those up there on that board, the 14-18 War and the innocent, just... caught up, the kids. (holding the fossil) It drives you mad, you must do something for him, you must try and... and you fight and bash at it, you can't sleep or sit still, and they wind you up tighter and tighter - and then just when you can't take any more of it, you'll split, you'll crack apart - then comes... (no break in the flow)... have you seen her eyes, they've got this funny green colour in them, you know, they've started to look at you, you suddenly catch her looking at you out of the corner of them, then when she sees you look, she looks the other way, did you know that? - pretends she wasn't looking, but... (switch)...it's built into you like some bloody great fishhook and you can't...you can't...and that's why - (he comes as near as he ever does to looking at the file) - I worked with people all my life, look what I've done in thirty five years since I left here, and I'll tell you mate, for nothing, it goes like that (he snaps his fingers)... and you think - Well what's the point? - that must be it, but where is it, what's it all been for?... (very quiet but equally outpoured)... and she's got these eyes, they don't look sick, you know, just... fantastic, it's as if, as if...

(Silence)

GLANVILLE. Good God

(He has fallen asleep sitting up in his chair)

CELLY. He's asleep.

(Gulls outside. Cut to: closeup of the fossil, round his neck)

*(The children's bedroom. Stillness)

BRUNO. I saw the gull woman today. She had red eyes and a horrible old stick.

CATHY. Don't Bruno.

BRUNO. I did.

(Pause. PETTA moves restlessly, trying to sleep. They look across at her)

239

CATHY. What does she think about?

CLARE. I think it must've all been like a dream to her, before she started to come right - like seeing everything from far off. But now...

(Silence)

(beat) Is she sleeping?

(The moon, blurry behind clouds)

(PERRY and VINCENT, watching the moon)

PERRY. Tony Gallagher's Dad is up there.

VINCENT. On the moon?

PERRY. Yes. He's got a bit of it in his garage.

VINCENT. What's it like?

PERRY. Oh - just grey stuff. Makes an awful mess, his mum said it ruined the new carpets.

(Pause)

VINCENT. I'd like to go up there for my International Service.

PERRY. I wouldn't like that.

VINCENT. It'd be fun.

PERRY. But they're shifting all those things up there, aren't they? - to inside the moon. All the powerplants and huge computer banks - so it's better down here for people to live. Why would you want to go up there for four years?

VINCENT. (serious) I'd have a huge telescope and look down through all the glass roofs on Earth, watching the girls undress.

(Pause)

PERRY. (serious) Have you ever seen a girl with nothing on?

VINCENT. No.

PERRY. Crispin has. He said it was...

VINCENT. What?

PERRY. Very strange.

VINCENT. Strange?

PERRY. Very strange, he said.

(Pause)

VINCENT. But I suppose... when we're older...

CATHY. Do you - ever get afraid of the future?

CLARE. Afraid?

CATHY. ...all the things they're doing, all the machines and - it's all going to be so different. I just get frightened thinking about it.

CLARE. But it's only people.

CATHY. What -

CLARE. - there'll only ever be people, and what they want!

CATHY. But people can be so -

CLARE. - and when they have time to think and breathe and love their children, they'll want good things. Then they'll all sing, like the people out there.

BRUNO. What people?

CLARE. All the drowned people. In the sea. They sing.

BRUNO. Why do they sing?

CLARE. I don't know. But they do.

(Pause)

BRUNO. You're potty.

CATHY. Hey, look.

CLARE. What?

CATHY. Petta -

> (Closeshot of PETTA. She is asleep. Sea heard outside, fainter)

> *(Main room. TURK sits asleep. ANNA sits watching him. The other two have gone)

TURK. (suddenly starting awake) I must just see if -

ANNA. The children are looking after her.

TURK. But she -

ANNA. She's asleep, so it doesn't matter, does it?

TURK. Asleep?

ANNA. (nods) Mm.

TURK. What, the...

ANNA. - little girl, yes.

TURK. Petta.

> (Pause)

> How long have I been...

ANNA. Not long. Come to bed.

TURK. I must just -

ANNA. Sleep. It's someone else's job now.

> *(Corner of hall)

GLANVILLE. So I haven't any option, have I?

CELLY. And Turk?

GLANVILLE. It'll happen to me too, someday.

> (He puts the file away in his briefcase and zips it up.

> *Main room)

242

ANNA. Those kids will be alright. Now the fighting's over, they'll keep them there - they've got the money now, to build special villages for them - away from where the fighting was. They can do that in six days now, a complete village. As Glan says that'll be better for them, won't it? (she notices him) Turk?

(He is asleep again. CELLY enters from the hall. ANNA signals to her to be quiet)

ANNA. He woke up for a moment.

CELLY. He's restless even now.

ANNA. (nods)

CELLY. Shall we move him?

ANNA. No, he might wake.

(TURK murmurs in his sleep)

CELLY. Look at him. That's not rest.

ANNA. (quietly) He won't - let - go.

CELLY. You'll stay with him?

ANNA. Yes. Pass me those rugs. There.

(She puts them round him. Then round herself)

Look at him. Like an old child. Oh, if I could rub those lines away with my fingers, he'd be twenty.

CELLY. He'll sleep now.

ANNA. He'll sleep.

(CELLY kisses him)

CELLY. Say goodbye to him for us. We'll creep out early. We've a lot to do.

(She goes out. ANNA sits there, watching TURK sleep. Fade)

(Fade up. The children's bedroom: day. Pan along row
of sleeping children, to PETTA at the end. She is sitting
up, examining her hands and navel with fascination./ BRUNO
mutters and crawls awake. He gets out of bed, PETTA
watching him./He crosses to toys and extracts a toy
trumpet. The house is silent and asleep. He puts it to
his lips, fills his lungs, and blows...

The beach. A white cloud of gulls flurries up, squawking;
CLARE and the others run after them, BRUNO tooting his
trumpet./ PETTA lollops along after them, both arms held
high above her head, squeaking with delight./Another cloud
of birds soars up.

TURK's bedroom. TURK slowly wakes)

TURK. What - how did I get here?

ANNA. We carried you. The kids and -

TURK. Carried?

ANNA. You walked, well sort of walked. You didn't wake up.

TURK. Uh. (looks round) Sun.

ANNA. Yes.

TURK. Where are they now?

ANNA. Out somewhere.

TURK. All of them?

ANNA. (nods) Together.

TURK. (takes this in) Uh. (rocks head) I feel so...

ANNA. Hush.

TURK. What? (sitting up abruptly) I'm not ill, you know,
    there's no point in treating me like I was - ugh! (head)

ANNA. OK, alright, relax; go on, lie back.

TURK. I must - just -

    (He swings out of bed and stands up)

- <u>where</u> are they?

*(Thick clump of bushes. The kids wandering and singing through thick bushes of sloe and bramble and gorse. CLARE and PETTA are apart. Bright sunlight)

BRUNO. Will she ever talk?

CATHY. Oh yes, she'll talk.

BRUNO. What will she say?

CATHY. All sorts of things.

BRUNO. Will she?

(CLARE singing away in background)

VINCENT. Look, here's more, oh, masses! -

PERRY. Don't eat them!

VINCENT. Gee, look Perry, hundreds - blackberries and peppers and those little red things, oh!

PERRY. Starting to turn, too, so in a few weeks... any little strawberries?

VINCENT. Oh, the sun's hot!

PERRY. Hot!

BRUNO. I like her, she's nice.

CATHY. She's beautiful.

BRUNO. Is she?

CATHY. Oh yes, she's got a beautiful face.

BRUNO. But no hair.

CATHY. Oh, she's got some. And it'll grow.

(VINCENT joins in singing with CLARE)

BRUNO. If I married her when I was big, what would happen?

245

PERRY. There'd be a loud explosion.

BRUNO. No, really, really Cathy?

CATHY. You'd have brown children.

BRUNO. But she's black.

C∠THY. Well, you're white.

BRUNO. So they'd be brown?

(VINCENT sings away quietly and happily in the background)

CLARE. (with PETTA) See that Petta? - ants, see? - hundreds of them, running along that line. Their nest is in there and they're getting food for it from by those flowers, see those little flowers? They move the earth - that lets in the air too, so the plants get it and grow better. Earthworms do that, too, and berries drop into the holes. There used to be butterflies, but they all died. I've seen pictures of them, but they all died. There were chemicals and things the farmers put down to kill things. They've stopped that now. But there's no butterflies; they all died.

(Vincent singing still)

PERRY. ...great fat sloes, look, and blackberries this year, look, see Cathy? Just turning, starting to turn...

*(TURK and ANNA coming through gorse clumps)

ANNA. Don't call.

TURK. No.

ANNA. Just - see her with them, that's all.

TURK. (stops) There's someone singing.

ANNA. Clare.

TURK. Yes, but there's more than one, it sounds like a lot, a lot of people. Perhaps...

ANNA. Mm?

(Silence)

246

TURK. Look at them.

(They watch. ANNA glances at him)

ANNA. Maybe it was your... job to get her <u>started</u>, just started. She's been with them lots of times.

TURK. (stares at her)

ANNA. Well of course she has.

TURK. I've been...

ANNA. - working, yes, I know.

(Pause. They walk)

TURK. She needs <u>me</u>.

ANNA. Sooner or later, there'll just be you.

TURK. Just be... ?

ANNA. You. Us.

(A rabbit hares away from under their feet)

(scream) Oh -

TURK. It's alright -

ANNA. Oh, it gave me...

TURK. - only a rabbit.

ANNA. Oh! (she laughs)

(Pause. Gulls)

TURK. Look -

ANNA. Mm?

TURK. Look at this.

(Rubble and low stone work, the overgrown remains of Old Romney church, covered in bushes and creepers. TURK stares at it.

*(VINCENT and BRUNO picking and eating unripe black-
berries, chatting away. Some way off, PERRY is la-la-ing
the little five note tune. PETTA, wandering about, is moving
to it, a lax but jerky dance. CATHY and CLARE watch)

CATHY. There's something still. Making her all... (gestures)

CLARE. Yes.

CATHY. Is it the blanket?

CLARE. Mm?

CATHY. She clutches it so tightly, all her muscles tense up -
that's why she moves so funny and jerky. Isn't it?

CLARE. I thought perhaps she'd...been through so much, seen
so much - (she avoids the word)

(They watch her)

CATHY. She'll be alright though.

CLARE. Yes?

CATHY. Don't you think?

CLARE. There was - so - much - death...

CATHY. (silence)

CLARE. And that's not part, is it? - not part of things.

(Pause)

(PETTA has stopped, half behind a bush)

CATHY. What's she doing?

CLARE. She's found something. Vincent - can you see what
it is that... (BRUNO yells)

CATHY. Someone there!

BRUNO. Clare!

*(The overgrown ruins of tiny church: they are about 100 yards

from the children)

TURK. (sitting on stone) I should have brought her <u>here</u>.

ANNA. Why?

TURK. Oh...

(Pause. It is more sheltered here: crickets and bees can be heard)

ANNA. You came before.

TURK. Just the once since I left here when I was twenty - when we moved back here, before the kids were born. That's when I got that board, you know? -

ANNA. The which?

TURK. Over my desk, with the names on it.

ANNA. Oh yes. You knew them.

TURK. No, no, before I was born. I found one bit here, under this stone, and another there and the third over there. All split apart so's you wouldn't have known what it was unless you'd seen it in one piece. There's one bit I never found. Nearly all the paint gone. Used to hang up there (points) on the wall. They were people killed in the war, y'know, the first war.

ANNA. Four of them.

TURK. There was a verse underneath, too, almost gone, can only read the beginning.

ANNA. Yes.

TURK. 'The last enemy...'. It's from the Bible, like you get on tombstones. And means about as much.

ANNA. No, it's death, isn't it?

TURK. Mm?

ANNA. Death, death's the last enemy.

TURK. Yes, well...

249

ANNA. 'The last enemy that shall be overcome is death'.

TURK. (beat) You know what I reckon's the worst thing about...
that? You'd never know what happened - who won or anything,
how it all turned out. They didn't did they? - never knew
if they done any good - all they knew was the fighting, then
suddenly - (gesture: pause) It's so... well, it's it, isn't it -
that's it.

ANNA. But perhaps... if other people achieve what they were
fighting for... then...

(Silence)

TURK. Mm?

ANNA. - in the future...

(TURK sits there, head down, the fossil in his hand. Gulls
heard.)

*(The children silently looking down at something below
camera./Close shot on an incredibly old woman, dressed in
rags and wrapped in an old black blanket: her face lined
and skinny like an old chicken./She lies in the sun on a tiny
patch of grass protected on three sides by thick bramble./
They look down at her: she looks beadily back)

WOMAN. Eh?

PERRY. Are you - are you alright?

WOMAN. (chuckles and hums, beady eyes taking them all in)

CATHY. Lift her head, let's get this under it - careful -

VINCENT. Here -

PERRY. You feeling alright?

(Silence. CATHY uncertainly feels her head and pulse. The
OLD WOMAN watches her. CATHY thinks a minute)

CATHY. Vincent, run back to the house and phone for a doctor.
Hurry.

(VINCENT runs off. For some reason,this amuses the OLD
WOMAN greatly. She grins and shudders with mirth,

250

clucking and humming. They all stare at her)

BRUNO. (who has crept close) You're very old, aren't you?

CLARE. Bruno!

BRUNO. How old are you? Are you a hundred?

(She clucks her tongue like a parrot, watching him)

I'm six!

WOMAN. (in mock admiration) Oh!

BRUNO. But I'm not afraid of you.

WOMAN. No no. Not afraid. Ha...!

(All the children creep closer to her. She watches them, grinning and clucking delightedly)

Yourn? (turns to CLARE and repeats) Yourn?

CLARE. Pardon?

(She points a skinny finger at PETTA)

Adopted. Sister.

WOMAN. Oh! Prutty! Ha!

BRUNO. Do you live here?

WOMAN. Er...er... (mumbles)

BRUNO. Where?

WOMAN. Live here...part of here, I'm the gull woman, heh heh.

BRUNO. But you're - ordinary!

WOMAN. (delighted) Yes! Ha! (this seems to delight her, and she goes off into an ecstasy of whistles, clucks and hums) - I am! Very old, heh heh...

(BRUNO pushes right in close to her)

BRUNO. (great concern) And is your Time Nearly Come?

WOMAN. S'pose it is. Yes. Tis. My time... heh -

(She is treating him with gentle adult seriousness, peering
at him down her bony beaked nose)

BRUNO. And are you sad?

WOMAN. Oh no. No. I've had a good life. No, I'm not sad.
Part of things, innit? (to PETTA) Prutty girlie, nice,
heh - (she puts out a gnarled hand and touches her cheek)

PETTA. (quite naturally) Pet. Ta.

WOMAN. Yes. Ha. (grins at her)

PETTA. Pet-ta.

WOMAN. Heh heh. Go 'way, cloud. Go 'way. Ah, there, there
she go. Sun. Blessed sun. Oh feel that ol' sun, is good,
innit. Well now - (with a contented sigh) - that's it then.

(And she dies, with infinite slowness, naturalness and
contentment, as if drifting off into sleep. The children
watch, crouched in a silent group around her. We see them
close - calm and fascinated at the beauty and naturalness
of it. They crouch there, silent, a long time after she has
died)

   *(Ruins of church)

ANNA. (quiet) Look -

TURK. What?

ANNA. (points)

(Some way off, PETTA can be seen close to thick bushes,
doing her gawky dance - but now slow, grave, graceful.
TURK starts to stand up)

ANNA. Stay here.

TURK. The others...

ANNA. They're there, see, by the bush? - you can half see them.

TURK. Yes.

252

(They watch)

ANNA. Clare taught her that.

TURK. She's - gentle, look.

ANNA. Yes.

TURK. She used to be - jerky, you know, when she...

ANNA. That's something else you could... that's something else.

TURK. Mm?

ANNA. (very close) You've been sick too. (pause) You must be gentle, gentle, to be strong.

(Mix to: CATHY, CLARE, BRUNO and PERRY around the OLD WOMAN, staring down at her. Behind them, PETTA moves gently in her dance.

Slow mix to: gulls in flight, seen very high up - smooth and steady in a cloudless sky.

Slow mix to: PETTA doing her slow grave dance, at the water's edge. CLARE stands beside her, PERRY hums the tune. The others watch, crouched down on their haunches. TURK and ANNA are heard over this)

TURK. (voice over) Good?

ANNA. (voice over) Oh, good. Stay there, stay still a minute. Oh...

(BRUNO starts quietly clapping to the tune: CATHY sways to it)

Remember the first time?

TURK. (voice over) Yes.

ANNA. (voice over) The clocks stopped.

TURK. (voice over) The sun...

ANNA. (voice over) - and the poppies, remember? - the huge red poppies in the field?

253

(PERRY sings the tune. VINCENT taps his feet, then starts moving to it)

TURK. (voice over) (lurching) Oh - er...oh...

ANNA. (voice over) Whatever are you doing?

TURK. (voice over) I just - that's better - got some stone or other in my kneecap.

ANNA. (voice over) Well, you will pick such places!

TURK. (voice over) Don't believe in wasting time. Oh - another bit - ugh!

(Creaks and groans: they are both heard to dissolve into helpless giggles.

CATHY starts to sing, CLARE to sway to the music. PETTA is dancing more confidently, but still gravely, gravely.

Close shot of TURK and ANNA, their heads close together and on the ground, just seen through the thick bushes. The children's singing continues behind)

ANNA. Oh feel, feel that sun! Do you reckon it's the first time - here?

TURK. Oh no.

ANNA. It's my first time here.

TURK. There was a Mrs. Stanley -

ANNA. And you never told me.

TURK. Not me. Anyhow, it's a long story.

ANNA. But - here?

TURK. Right here. Just about there, to be exact. I'll put up a plaque.

ANNA. What will it say?

TURK. (after thought) "Whoopee".

ANNA. (giggles)

254

(Helicopter slowly descending on the marsh, by bushes. Kids singing continues behind)

TURK. (voice over) That was on a Sunday too. Like us.

ANNA. (voice over) Oh yes, our first -

TOGETHER. (voice over) - time was on a Sunday!

(Pause)

TURK. (voice over) Easter Island.

(Cut to: a covered stretcher being lifted up and carried to waiting helicopter in bushes)

ANNA. (voice over) The huge red poppies in that field.

TURK. (voice over) Flanders Poppies, they were.

ANNA. (voice over) Were they?

TURK. (voice over) Flanders Poppies.

(The children sing, still quiet. VINCENT joins in la-la-ing the tune and clapping)

TURK. (voice over) I thought of going to church instead, but I'd forgotten my hymnbook.

ANNA. (voice over) Perhaps we should have anyway.

TURK. (voice over) Oh aye. Or after.

ANNA. (voice over) Oh, not after, I couldn't have moved. Could you?

TURK. (voice over) Oh, I could, yes. But I would have sung all the time.

ANNA. (voice over) Sung?

TURK. (voice over) Oh yes -

(The helicopter takes off and lifts high up into the air)

- out loud. You know how it takes me.

ANNA. (voice over) Oh aye, I do remember. Just.

TURK. (voice over) Uh - that's enough. That's past.

ANNA. (voice over) Ordinary people are content to sing after
their bath or something, but you...!

TURK. (voice over) Lay off, it's natural.

ANNA. (voice over) For you maybe. Made it very awkward at
times. Unromantic. Just when you want to lie there, you
start to... laugh!

(Pan down from the helicopter to PETTA's blanket, lying by
the crushed grass where the GULL WOMAN died. The
children sing behind.

The church ruin)

TURK. There was a chap lived here you know - used to sing.

ANNA. What...?

TURK. No, all the time.

ANNA. Oh?

TURK. Specially when he was with people. Dotty-happy he was,
used to sing all the time in church here, and laugh, you know,
right through the prayers and sermon and everything. Very
loudly, deafening at times.

ANNA. Why did he do that?

TURK. He was happy I suppose. Made it very difficult to do
anything, you know.

(The children on the beach, dancing and singing quietly)

ANNA. (voice over) What did he sing?

TURK. (voice over) Oh everything - opera, national anthem, the
pops - you know... they used to try and shut him out when they
saw him coming Sunday mornings but he'd just stand outside
and sing twice as loud - oh that loud. Mad-happy he was,
glorious. It can take you that way, you know, sometimes?

ANNA. (voice over) What can?

TURK. (voice over) (laughs) Don't you know?

(PETTA lifts her arms and dances gravely, freely)

ANNA. (voice over) Oh, look at the moon!

TURK. (voice over) Oh aye.

ANNA. (voice over) But what's it doing out in the daylight?

TURK. (voice over) It often is.

ANNA. (voice over) No it isn't, it can't be!

TURK. (voice over) It is, of course it is!

ANNA. (voice over) And look - isn't that a star there, see? - by that cloud, that's a star isn't it?

TURK. (voice over) No, not stars in the daytime -

ANNA. (voice over) It is! It is!

TURK. (laughs)

ANNA. (voice over) You've started!

TURK. (voice over - creaking with laughter) I can't help it!

ANNA. (voice over) Stop it, stop it! - you've started see? - so unromantic!

TURK. (voice over) - can't help it! It was his trouble too.

ANNA. (voice over) (starting to gurgle with laughter herself) That man?

TURK. (voice over) Yes!

ANNA. (voice over) What was - what was his trouble?

TURK. (voice over) (barely getting it out for laughing) - Love!

(PETTA dances slow, grave.

Cut to the helicopter, now a faint dot in the sky across the marshes.

There comes the faint murmur of countless voices, joining in

257

singing the tune with the children, quietly, just audibly.

Cut to the children dancing, from further off.

Cut to low shot, swooping with a gull low over the water. The singing continues.

Mix to: high wide shot of the beach and the water's edge, and the sea to the horizon. PETTA and the other children seen bottom frame./ The singing, quiet and gentle, and joining in the children's song, rises steadily from the enormity of the sea. Fade)

PROGRAMME OF THE TRILOGY

Each play deals with one of the three key turning points in Turk's life. He is never the main protagonist, but catalyst and observer. The central figure of Play I is Old'Un; of Play II, the whole group; and of Play III, the children.

The first play is the breakup of the old order; the middle play, the search for new values; the last play, society starting to acquire them and launching forward on a new basis.

Also: Play I is the slow death of the Almighty "up there" - separate to man, a separate Authority - the one gigantic eye of the mural disclosed in the final disintegration being part of the face of this God revealed, and lifeless; working by degrees (as trying to mend and get through by radio to find direction in Play II) through to the end of Play III - God is within man and working through him (the children).

The crux and pivot of the whole trilogy is the first Bikini H-Bomb test in 1954, and passing through the fallout. Just as a man, consciously passing close to death (as Turk does with his injury, and as their mini-society does with the fallout) re-emerges on the other side (if he does) to some degree changed, more responsible, never taking life for granted again, but prizing it in magnificence; so also a society doing the same - as ours is now, and has been since 1945 - could re-emerge better and more responsible and humane than ever before, precisely because of our present closeness to the brink.

Play I is the Flood slowly coming in and covering the earth; Play II, they are in the Ark, riding the waters and seeking the way to Mount Ararat; Play III, the waters have subsided, the Ark is now a rusting shell on the seashore where it grounded, and new land is being created by the receding sea.

The Captain in the middle play is a macabre shadow of Old'un in the first play, a mummified tendon of a man, the sad and ghostly remnant of Authority. He is Death, almost the mediaeval morality-figure, attempting to take charge of their groping society.

This character continues into the last play as the Gullwoman, now without even a ghost-vestige of Authority; she is the personification of death; and she is the one thing the central characters of this play - the children - cannot accept or understand. This is seen most clearly in the behaviour of the most sensitive member of their little society, Clare. It is their ultimate acceptance of death into the scheme of things that is the final act of healing in the trilogy.

C AND B PLAYSCRIPTS

		Cloth	Paper
*PS 1	TOM PAINE by Paul Foster	21s	9s0d
*PS 2	BALLS and other plays (The Recluse, Hurrah for the Bridge The Hessian Corporal) by Paul Foster	25s	10s0d
PS 3	THREE PLAYS (Lunchtime Concert, Coda The Inhabitants) by Olwen Wymark	21s	7s0d
*PS 4	CLEARWAY by Vivienne C. Welburn	21s	7s0d
*PS 5	JOHNNY SO LONG and THE DRAG BY Vivienne C. Welburn	25s	9s0d
*PS 6	SAINT HONEY and OH DAVID, ARE YOU THERE? by Paul Ritchie	25s	11s0d
PS 7	WHY BOURNEMOUTH? and other plays (The Missing Links, An Apple a Day) by John Antrobus	25s	10s0d
*PS 8	THE CARD INDEX and other plays (The Interrupted Act, Gone Out) by Tadeusz Rozewicz trans. Adam Czerniawski	25s	11s0d
PS 9	US by Peter Brook and others	42s	21s0d
*PS 10	SILENCE and THE LIE by Nathalie Sarraute trans. Maria Jolas	25s	9s0d
*PS 11	THE WITNESSES and other plays (The Old Woman Broods, The Funny Old Man) by Tadeusz Rozewicz trans. Adam Czerniawski	25s	9s0d

		Cloth	Paper
*PS 24	PRECIOUS MOMENTS FROM THE FAMILY ALBUM TO PROVIDE YOU WITH COMFORT IN THE LONG YEARS TO COME by Naftali Yavin	25s	9s0d
*PS 25	DESIRE CAUGHT BY THE TAIL by Pablo Picasso trans. Roland Penrose	18s	8s0d
*PS 26	THE BREASTS OF TIRESIAS by Guillaume Apollinaire	18s	8s0d
PS 27	ANNA LUSE and other plays (Jens, Purity) by David Mowat	30s	15s0d
*PS 28	O and other plays by Sandro Key-Aarberg	30s	15s0d
*PS 29	WELCOME TO DALLAS MR. KENNEDY by Kaj Himmelstrup	25s	9s0d
PS 30	THE LUNATIC, THE SECRET SPORTSMAN AND THE WOMEN NEXT DOOR and VIBRATIONS by Stanley Eveling	30s	12s0d
*PS 31	STRINDBERG by Colin Wilson	21s	9s0d
*PS 32	THE FOUR LITTLE GIRLS by Pablo Picasso trans. Roland Penrose	25s	10s0d
PS 33	MACRUNE'S GUEVARA by John Spurling	25s	9s0d
*PS 34	THE MARRIAGE by Witold Gombrowicz trans. Louis Iribarne	35s	15s0d
*PS 35	BLACK OPERA and THE GIRL WHO BARKS LIKE A DOG by Gabriel Cousin trans. Irving Lycett	30s	15s0d

*PS 49	THE NUTTERS and other plays (Social Service, A Cure for Souls) by A.F. Cotterell	25s	10s0d
PS 50	THE GYMNASIUM and other plays (The Technicians, Stay Where You Are, Jack the Giant-Killer) by Olwen Wymark	25s	10s0d
PS 51	THE MAN IN THE GREEN MUFFLER and other plays (In Transit, The Sword) by Stewart Conn	25s	10s0d
*PS 52	CALCIUM and other plays (Coins, The Good Shine, Broken, Victims) by Jan Quackenbush	25s	10s0d
*PS 53	FOUR BLACK REVOLUTIONARY PLAYS (Experimental Death Unit 1, A Black Mass, Great Goodness of Life, Madheart) by Leroi Jones	25s	10s0d
PS 54	LONG VOYAGE OUT OF WAR by Ian Curteis	42s	21s0d
PS 55	INUIT and THE OTHERS by David Mowat	25s	10s0d
PS 56	COUNCIL OF LOVE by Oscar Panizza trans. and adapted by John Bird	30s	12s0d
PS 57	CURTAINS by Tom Mallin	30s	12s0d

*All plays marked thus are represented for dramatic presentation by:
C and B (Theatre) Ltd, 18 Brewer Street London W1